Darryl M.

# CORE VALUES
## FOR THE
# YOUNG
(and Not So Young)
# CHRISTIAN

insight
PUBLISHING GROUP

*Core Values for the Young (and Not So Young) Christian*
© 2010 by Darryl M. Bloodworth

Published by Insight Publishing Group
4739 E. 91st Street, Suite 210
Tulsa, OK 74137
918-493-1718

Unless otherwise noted all Scripture quotations are taken from the New Revised Standard Version Bible, copyright © 1989 by the Division of Christian Education of the National Council of the Churches of Christ in the United States of America, and the NRSV Reference Bible with Apocrypha, copyright © 1993 by Zondervan Publishing House, Grand Rapids, Michigan 49530

Excerpts from *The Message of the Sermon on the Mount* © 1978 by John R.W. Stott, Published by InterVarsity Press, Rights and Permissions Department, Post Office Box 1400, Downers Grove, Illinois 60515.

Excerpts from William Barclay, *The Gospel of Matthew,* Vol. One, Westminster John Knox Press, 100 Witherspoon Street, Louisville, Kentucky 40202-1396.

Excerpts from *Prayer: Finding the Heart's True Home,* copyright © 1992 by Richard J. Foster, HarperCollins Publishers, 10 East 53rd Street, New York, New York 10022.

ISBN: 978-1-932503-92-0

Library of Congress catalog card number: 2010929787

Printed in the United States of America

# ENDORSEMENTS

"This book is a deeply Biblical, practical and compelling guide to life. The stories and teaching are engaging because they are so true for us all."

Dr. Joel C. Hunter, Senior Pastor
Northland - A Church Distributed

"Humanists have often charged the beatitudes with being theoretical and impractical. They are, of course, neither and in this book, Bloodworth gives them legs to run on and hands to work with."

Mark Rutland, Ph.D
President, Oral Roberts University

"During high school, I was a member of a Sunday School class in which Darryl Bloodworth taught on the Sermon on the Mount and on core values. As a result of taking his class I feel that I have a better understanding of Jesus' teaching and the life that Jesus calls us to live as his followers. Now that I am in college, I still observe my behavior and ask myself if I actually exhibit the core values that I profess as a Christian. Having knowledge of core values before entering a new life in college has really helped me to stay on track with my faith. Establishing your core values, getting into the practice of examining your behavior and living out your core values before you are challenged has the potential to keep you from difficult situations, and, more importantly, brings us closer to our Savior through living as he instructs us to."

Janelle Lyons

# DEDICATION

To my family—Inez, Mary, Krista, David and Joey—my inspiration for writing this book.

# CONTENTS

# PREFACE

The years between ages 15 and 30 are years during which most people make decisions that will shape and direct most of the rest of their lives. Decisions are made about whether to go to college, and if so, where; what career field to pursue; what person to marry; whether to begin a family; what part of the country to live in, and many other life changing decisions.

Additionally, these are some of the most important years of character formation. Admittedly, character formation begins long before the mid-teens, but it usually solidifies during ages 15-30. Character traits formed during this critical period of life do not easily change thereafter. It is possible to change one's character after age 30 but it becomes increasingly difficult.

Furthermore, mistakes made during these years may change the course of one's life. An impulsive decision to shoplift or to get drunk and drive may ruin an otherwise bright future and bring untold regret and suffering not only to the person making those decisions but to others as well, not least the person's family. An unplanned pregnancy can change a young woman's life immediately, and perhaps the young man's life as well. Cheating may result in a student being expelled from college, leaving a legacy that will be with that person for the rest of his or her life. Unless young men and young women have thought through the decisions they are likely to face on issues such as cheating, drugs, sex and alcohol, to name a few, they will be ill prepared to make wise choices when confronted with such issues, particularly in the midst of significant peer pressure.

By the age of 40, we can look back over our lives and track how the decisions that we have made in life have led us to the point at which we then find ourselves. This is one reason turning 40 is so traumatic for many people. Unfortunately, there is very little instruction for young people (or older people for that matter) on how to make wise decisions in life. They receive plenty of instruction on how to read, how to do math, how to do a host of other things, but very little on how to make real life decisions. Most of the training that one receives on how to make decisions comes from the home, or perhaps the church. However, as we look about us we find that even children raised in Christian families make their share of bad decisions. And attending church is no guarantee that the young man or woman will make any better decisions than those who do not go to church.

The fact is that we have done a rather poor job in our culture of preparing our children to make the kinds of difficult decisions that they will have to make during the early part of their lives. Unfortunately, we in the church have not done much better than the culture in general to prepare our children to make these tough decisions. This is particularly sad because Jesus had much to say about how we are to live our lives and the values that should shape our decisions in life.

This book is the product of a Sunday School class that I taught for teenagers for about 10 years. The course upon which this book is based was designed to help the students, all young Christians, come to understand and incorporate into their character the values that Jesus taught. Once these values become our "core values," as explained in this book, we will have a solid foundation upon which to make decisions in life. These values will become the core of our character and ultimately help define who we are as individuals.

If you are interested in developing your character to be the kind of person God wants you to be, this book should be helpful. It is directed to young people who have already made a decision to be a Christian. However, if you have not yet made such a decision, the book will help you understand what it means to be a Christian; it should also help you decide whether you want to become a Christian.

Finally, if you are over 30 you will still find this book helpful in making decisions day by day. The development of Christian character does not end at age 30, and neither does the need to make good decisions. Furthermore, this book may help you develop within your own children or grandchildren the core values and character they will need to safely navigate through the decisions with which they will be confronted. There is no finer legacy that you could leave them.

Darryl M. Bloodworth

# ACKNOWLEDGEMENTS

This book would not have been possible without the help of many people. First, I want to thank my beautiful wife, Mary, for her love, strong support and encouragement to keep writing when, at times, I became discouraged. She is a far better writer than I am and her editing always improved the final product. My assistant, friend and critic, Natalie Buckner, not only critiqued and edited each chapter as it was written but provided research and offered many awesome insights that I had simply never thought of. Without her able assistance, this book would never have come to fruition. But most of all I want to thank the students who were in my Sunday School class. As we explored the scriptures together, their questions and comments challenged me to dig deeper into the words of Jesus in the Sermon on the Mount, and other scriptures, and to learn how to internalize them to the point of becoming core values. I learned far more from the class than they ever did, and I will always be grateful for the times we had together learning the core values that Jesus taught.

# CHAPTER 1

# INTRODUCTION TO CORE VALUES

### *Why do our lives turn out the way they do?*

Charles Browne rolled over on his cot and stared at the ceiling through the dim light of his prison cell. He had been trying to go to sleep for over an hour, but sleep would not come. His first month in prison had been difficult. The days were so miserable that he looked forward to lights out at 10:00 P.M. so he could retreat into his own little world in his cell. He just wanted to get lost in sleep and ignore the harsh, ugly world about him. But each night followed the same pattern. He would try to fall asleep, but the harder he tried the more sleep eluded him. Instead, he would see in his mind's eye his wife and four-year-old daughter crying and looking at him with a pained, disbelieving expression as he left home to begin a 28-month prison sentence. That picture had been seared into his memory and Charles could not dislodge it until sleep would mercifully come well into another lonely night.

Tonight, however, his thoughts wandered back to his childhood. Charles remembered his childhood fondly. He had grown up in a Christian family in a suburban community. The church that he and his family attended was only two blocks from his home. He recalled his life being centered around family, church and school.

1

Charles had been a good student. In fact, he was smart enough that he seldom studied in high school, but made good grades anyway. Getting good grades was important to Charles because he looked forward to attending a good college and preparing for a professional career as an accountant or lawyer. As he thought back to those days, however, he remembered that there were times that his lack of preparation left him unprepared for tests or for completing a research paper on time. On more than one occasion he had cheated from a classmate's paper, or used another student's research to complete his term paper. At the time, that did not seem to be a big deal. It was just one test. Why should he risk his grade point average when he could get away with cheating without being caught?

As he thought more about his childhood, one night in particular stood out. He was 15 years old and was attending the Youth Fellowship meeting at his church. The youth director, Max Johnson, was urging Charles and the other 15-year-olds to think and pray about their future. Charles recalled Mr. Johnson saying something that Charles found quite surprising. Mr. Johnson said that God was interested in all aspects of our lives, not just our time at church. Charles had not thought of that before, but it made sense to him. Mr. Johnson also told them that they could use their talents and gifts to fulfill their potential and also to serve God at the same time. This, too, made sense to Charles. For the first time he began to realize that what he wanted to do after college was become a CPA and perhaps be the chief financial officer of a small business, as his father was. Charles felt full of promise that night. He was confident that this is what he wanted to do, and he promised Mr. Johnson that he would pray about his future. But Charles now realized he didn't follow up on that promise to pray about his future; in fact Charles could not remember praying about much of anything except for the next test, particularly when he hadn't studied. Charles also remembered that he continued to cheat from time to time.

Charles' good grades got him into the college he wanted and he thoroughly enjoyed college life. It was a bit of a wild time for Charles. Whereas church and family had been a significant part of his life in high school, during college Charles was more interested in partying and enjoying his freedom. His social life, however, interfered with his study time. His grades were OK, but nowhere near his potential. In fact, his grades would not have been as good as they were if he had not continued to cheat on some of his more significant research papers. By now, Charles wasn't particularly proud of the fact he cheated on some of his major papers, but to him the end justified the means. He was determined to graduate, become a CPA and get the job he was looking for.

Charles finished college with respectable grades, and, to his surprise, passed the CPA examination on the first attempt, something few accountants achieved. Best of all, he landed a job as assistant comptroller at a small but growing business in the electronics field. The pay wasn't great initially, but times were tough, and Charles was happy to have a job. He felt that he had a promising future with the company.

Shortly after Charles began working for the company, he began dating Carol and they soon decided that they wanted to get married. Charles and Carol had similar backgrounds; they had both grown up in the same suburb, and they both wanted to live the life of understated affluence that their parents had lived. Living in the right neighborhood was very important to them, and within a few years after they were married they found the perfect house, not far from where both of them had grown up. It was more house than they needed, and more than they could really afford, but they knew they would be happy in that house. Besides, housing prices always went up, right? They were concerned that if they did not buy the house now, they may never be able to afford it.

So they bought the house, and soon enough the cost of it began to weigh on Charles and Carol. They always seemed to be broke. Although Charles' income was going up, it wasn't going up fast enough, especially when Carol got pregnant and was no longer bringing in a salary. After living under financial strain for several years, Charles discovered that he could supplement his income by slightly padding his expense account. He had to travel frequently in his job, and he found ways to add phantom expenses to his reimbursement forms. Nothing significant. Just enough to help Charles and Carol keep up with their ever increasing expenses in their new house and nice neighborhood.

Charles justified fudging his expense account because all the travel was taking him away from his family, and the false expenses were nothing significant. At least they were not large at first. But after a few years Charles found that he could submit larger phantom expenses and then create false journal entries in the books of the company to hide those expenses. Since he was creating the monthly financial statements for the company he was always able to make offsetting journal entries that covered the monies he was taking. He knew this was wrong, just as he had known his cheating was wrong, but he rationalized what he was doing because it was important to him that his family have the home and neighborhood they had. And there were always new expenses, new reasons for helping himself to company money, and expertly covering it up.

As Charles' eyes began to adjust to the dank, grey walls around him, the harsh reality of the last few months came back to him. An IRS audit of the company's tax returns led to the discovery of Charles' embezzlement. The company had to pay not only back taxes but also huge penalties and interest to the IRS. Charles would never forget the shock on the face of the owner and CEO of the company when he learned that Charles had embezzled from the company. But as bad as that was, telling Carol what had happened was even worse. In her eyes he could see the same shame and disbelief he saw in his own eyes when he looked in the mirror.

Because the company had contracts with the county government, Charles' embezzlement quickly became public, and the State

Attorney's office filed criminal charges against Charles. His lawyer negotiated a plea deal for him that resulted in a 28-month sentence in the state penitentiary. Also, because he was now a convicted felon, his CPA license was revoked.

In the darkness of his prison cell the realization of what Charles had done to himself, to his family and to his friends at the company descended on him once again and he began to weep, silently at first, and then in stifled sobs. He still had 27 more months to serve in the penitentiary, and a life to somehow try to rebuild. As his sobs finally began to subside, he asked himself over and over "How did I get from that hopeful 15-year-old boy to a convicted 34-year-old felon? How could I lose my way so badly?"

At the same time Charles was facing the reality of what he had done to his life, Rachel Singleton was sitting in the small kitchen of her second floor, slightly shabby apartment having a cup of coffee and allowing herself the only few minutes of time she would have to herself all day. After only six hours of sleep she was bone tired, as she always seemed to be. She would have to get her two daughters up in another 20 minutes to get them dressed, fed and off to school. Janie was eight and struggling in the third grade; Susan was six and doing well academically in the first grade but was having some behavioral problems that Susan's teacher wanted to talk to her about. "How can I find time to help the girls in school?" Rachel wondered. That helpless feeling that at times overwhelmed her was coming back.

Rachel was working two jobs to support herself and the girls. She worked as a waitress at a diner from shortly after she dropped the girls off at school until time to pick them up. She would then take the girls to her mother's house which was only 15 minutes from her apartment. Her mother had been a life saver. She had agreed to keep the girls from after school until Rachel picked them up after her second job as a waitress and sometimes bartender at a popular restaurant downtown. Rachel hated having to work two jobs and be away from the girls so much but she needed both jobs just to make ends meet. The tips from the evening job had been a big help, but as the economic recession began to spread, the number of diners declined, and so did the tips.

As Rachel poured herself a second cup of coffee she mentally calculated how much she would need in tips over the next week to be able to buy the girls the fall clothes they would need as the weather turned cooler. There always seemed to be more needs than money.

Her thoughts wandered; she appreciated this time each morning, but increasingly felt sorry for herself. This isn't the way she thought her life was going to turn out. Although still only 30 and attractive, Rachel felt old and overwhelmed; it seemed life was passing her by. Through her rambling thoughts about her depressing situation Rachel remembered, of all things, her sixteenth birthday. It was on a Sunday. Her father was still alive then. He, her mother and Rachel had attended church, as they occasionally did, and then went out for lunch at their favorite restaurant, complete with a small birthday cake for Rachel.

What she remembered best about that day was the conversation with her parents. They treated her as an adult for what Rachel felt was the first time. They talked encouragingly about her future; she could become anything she wanted to be. It gave Rachel hope that she had not often felt about herself. She always had problems with self esteem, and often tried to overcome those feelings by having a boyfriend. Rachel's biggest fights with her parents were over her boyfriend, Roger. Her parents were concerned that she was becoming far too serious far too young with Roger. Rachel always told her parents that they were being old fashioned. Most of her friends were just as involved with their boyfriends as she was. Although she didn't tell her parents, Rachel knew that some of her friends were in a sexual relationship with their boyfriends. But Rachel knew her parents were right, and she told them she was going to avoid getting too serious with Roger. She intended to put more emphasis on her studies and attend college to become an elementary school teacher, a goal of hers since elementary school.

But Rachel did not follow through on her promise to her parents that day. Even on those occasions that she attended Sunday School with her best friend, Sally, and they discussed the Christian view of marriage, Rachel kept thinking that she was ready for a more adult relationship with a man long before she would finish college and get married.

And, so, during college Rachel wound up moving in with Roger. To Rachel, this was not just some youthful romance, but real love that she thought would eventually result in marriage. But it did not. Despite living together for three and a half years—including the year they both took off from college—Rachel and Roger broke up during their senior year in college. Roger dropped out of college and joined the Army. Rachel was so distraught by the breakup that she also dropped out of college. By the time Rachel learned she was pregnant Roger was already on his way to Iraq. Roger's response to Rachel's announcement that she was pregnant was initially encouraging. When he returned from Iraq, he wanted to resume the relationship and they would marry; Rachel would have what she always wanted, a family of her own. Rachel's dream, however, was not to be. Roger did return from Iraq, but not to Rachel. He suffered from mental and emotional problems from combat, and was not the same man Rachel had known before. Even though she asked him to come see his daughter after Janie was born, Roger never came, and he never showed any further interest in her or in Janie.

Within a year after Janie was born, Rachel met Steve, and they had a whirlwind romance. This time Rachel was sure she had found true love. Steve seemed to be emotionally supportive and sensitive to her. He also loved Janie. The fact that Steve never wanted to discuss long range plans did not seem all that critical to Rachel. She believed that in time he would be willing to make a commitment to her. Rachel began praying that Steve would not only love her but make a permanent commitment to her by marrying her. But after less than a year, Steve began to lose interest and finally announced to Rachel that he was moving to Colorado, and he was not taking her with him.

Once again, Rachel was crushed. And once again she discovered she was pregnant. By the time Susan was born, Rachel had not heard from Steve in six months.

As Rachel finished her coffee, she reminded herself how much she loved her girls. Although life was difficult for her and for the girls she was grateful for them. She could not imagine life without them. She just wished she had answers for their questions about why they did not have a father around as many of their friends did. And why did their fathers not care enough to come see them, especially on their birthday or at Christmas?

As Rachel arose to get Janie and Susan ready for school, she asked herself again, as she did almost every day, "How did I get from that hopeful 16-year-old girl to an unwed mother of two young girls? This is not where I thought I would be at 30."

## *Why do we make the decisions we make?*

Many people have asked the same question that Charles and Rachel asked themselves: How did I get to this point in life? This isn't where I thought I would be. Often the question is asked in disappointment; sometimes it is asked in anger, and we blame other people, circumstances, or even God, for the disappointments in our lives. After all, weren't we promised that if we make a commitment to Christ that he would bless us, both in this life and in the life to come?

The truth is that Jesus never promised that we would be blessed apart from him. In John 13:17 he said "If you know these things, you are blessed *if you do them*." Shortly thereafter, on the same night, he told his disciples "If you love me, you will keep my commandments." (John

14:15) "Just as the branch cannot bear fruit by itself unless it abides in the vine, neither can you unless you abide in me." (John 15:4)  Again and again Jesus emphasized obedience in his followers.  The obedience that Jesus seeks is not just in the big decisions in life but also in the small, sometimes mundane decisions that we make each day.

Why would Jesus be so interested in our constant obedience, in our abiding in him day by day?  Undoubtedly, it is because Jesus well knew that our lives are largely the result of the decisions we make over time. The path we take in life is determined not just by the big decisions we make but also by the little decisions that may seem unimportant at the time.  Jesus knew that without his being an active participant in those decisions we will fare no better than those who have never committed to the Christian life.  As always, Jesus was blunt with his disciples: "... apart from me you can do nothing." (John 15:5)

Yet we are reluctant to involve God in the decisions we make, except, perhaps, for some of the big decisions.  The problem is that after we have ignored God in the small decisions we make it is difficult to hear his voice when it is time for the big decisions.  The result is that our prayers regarding the big decisions are often little more than asking God to give us what we have already decided we want.  Rather than asking God for his direction in the big decisions of our lives we simply ask him to bless what we have already decided we are going to do.

Charles did not involve God in his decision to cheat in school or his decision to begin padding his expense account.  The years of cheating in school made it easier for him to begin cheating on his expenses.  Besides, claiming false expenses was no big deal, he thought; he wasn't hurting anyone by claiming expenses that he never incurred; other people were doing the same thing, and these were expenses he easily could have incurred, and for which he could have legitimately been reimbursed had he incurred them.  But by ignoring God in this little decision it was easier to ignore God as the size of his phantom expenses grew.  His little decisions to ignore God grew into big decisions to ignore God.

Rachel also failed to involve God in her relationship with Roger. Despite her commitment to her parents to cool her relationship with Roger, and despite her knowledge from Sunday School that living with a man before marriage was wrong, she decided that she was ready to move in with Roger even though she was not married to him. Furthermore, she repeated her mistake with Steve. Rather than learning from the painful mistakes of her first relationship, and committing to God to change her behavior (i.e., repent), she soon entered into another relationship similar to the one with Roger. Having ignored God when she moved in with Roger, it was easier to ignore God when Steve came along, especially in the midst of the overwhelming feeling that she had found "true love."

The problem that Charles and Rachel both had is that they—like many other professing Christians—never developed a strong set of internal values consistent with what Jesus taught to guide them through the large and the small decisions of life. Thus, their behavior was unrelated to what they purported to believe as Christians. It wasn't that they intended to be disobedient Christians; they just ignored what Jesus taught, either out of ignorance or because they were so self-centered that they gave little or no thought to what God wanted for their lives.

These internal values are what I have termed "core values." The purpose of this book is to examine the core values that Jesus taught and to suggest ways for you to develop strong Christian core values and live by them.

## *What are core values?*

The term "core values" is one used most often by institutions, such as universities, corporations or other organizations. When they talk about their core values they are referring to those values that control and direct their decisions and their strategic planning—those values that define who they are. My alma mater is the United States Air Force Academy. That institution is quite clear about its core values: "Integrity first; service before self; and excellence in all we do." As with any institution, it has not achieved perfection in living those values, but these are the values that it wants to instill in its graduates. And it measures its success largely by how well its graduates honor those values.

The term "core values" is not a Biblical term. I have not found it in any translation of the Bible, either in the Old Testament or the New Testament. Nevertheless, Jesus often addressed the core values of those who came to him. The rich young man (Matt. 19:16-26) came to Jesus asking what he must do to have eternal life. Jesus quickly gleaned that at the young man's core was his love of money. That value was the most important to him. He claimed that he had kept all of the commandments, and asked "What do I still lack?" But when Jesus asked him to give up that which he loved the most, he could not do it. Matthew says "He went away grieving, for he had many possessions."

In the parable of the prodigal son (Luke 15:11-32), Jesus focused on the love and compassion of the father for his younger son who spurned his father, wasted his inheritance and only repented when he had no choice but to return to his father or die. At the core of the father's being was his love for his son, and his compassion for him. These values were so strong that even the younger son's disrespectful behavior could not overcome them. The father's love and compassion, by comparison, stood in stark contrast with the cold anger of the older son who resented the forgiveness his younger brother received from their father.

In these Biblical stories the characters' behavior reflected the values that were at their core: in the rich young man, the love of money; in the father of the prodigal, love and compassion; and in the older brother, self-centeredness, anger and resentment. However, if someone asked the rich young man if the love of money was the strongest value he held, he would deny it. The older brother would deny that self-centeredness, anger and resentment were at the core of his relationship with his brother. He would justify himself by saying he only wanted what was fair. The point is this: we often are unaware of the core values that cause us to behave the way we do and cause us to make the decisions that we make. As we shall see, one of the most difficult, and most painful, things that we must do as we attempt to live the Christian life is to confront our own core values and to commit to God that we will allow him to change our values to the values that Jesus taught.

So, what are core values? As used in this book, core values are those values held deeply within us, either consciously or unconsciously, that cause us to make the decisions that we make. We may have many values that we say are important to us, but if those values do not affect our behavior they are not *core* values. Core values, by definition, are those values that affect our behavior. Sadly, many of the values that Jesus taught have never become core values for his followers.

Why are core values so important? Because they are like the rudder on a ship. A ship with a properly functioning rudder can be steered precisely, even in turbulent seas. On the other hand, a ship without a properly functioning rudder is at the mercy of the sea, and if that ship encounters a storm it may capsize.

One of the better known stories to come out of World War II was the story of the sinking of the Bismarck by the British Navy. The Bismarck was a German battleship commissioned in August 1940, during the early days of World War II. It was the largest warship then on the seas, and supposedly the greatest naval ship ever built. Indeed, the Bismarck sank the British battlecruiser HMS Hood, the most powerful ship in the British Navy, within several minutes of engaging Hood in May 1941 in the Denmark Strait. This caused British Prime Minister Winston Churchill to issue the famous order to "Sink the Bismarck." The problem was that the British Navy had no ship equal to the Bismarck. How the British Navy was able to sink the Bismarck is instructive.

The British launched a small number of Swordfish biplane torpedo bombers from an aircraft carrier to attempt to strike the Bismarck with a torpedo. Given the age and limited capabilities of these airplanes this was definitely a long shot, but in a final attack by one of the torpedo bombers as night was falling on the evening of May 26, 1941, a single torpedo hit the rudder of the Bismarck, jamming its rudder and steering gear. The Bismarck was then relatively helpless and was sunk by the British Navy within three hours of initiating the final attack the next morning. Without a functioning rudder, the greatest ship on the seas perished.

Just as the Bismarck was at the mercy of the British Navy once it lost its rudder, our lives can become badly off track if the rudder of our lives—our core values—does not function properly. For the Christian, our core values should be the values that Jesus taught. Part of what Jesus meant by saying that we must abide in him is that his values must become our values, and those are the values by which we must make the daily decisions of our lives.

### How do we know what someone's core values are?

Before we address how to determine what our core values are, as opposed to what we say they are, there are a few things we should acknowledge about core values.

First, everyone has core values, not just Christians. Second, core values can be good or they can be bad. Sometimes core values may even be neutral from a moral standpoint. Examples of good core values are truthfulness and loyalty. Bad core values include self-centeredness and no concern for the truth (causing one to be a liar). A somewhat neutral core value is the desire to be liked and accepted. Although the desire to be liked and accepted is normal and not bad in itself, it can lead to bad decisions and great harm if it overcomes other core values, such as honesty. One reason that cheating is so prevalent in our schools today is that many young people have a stronger desire to be liked and accepted than they do to be honest. So, they allow a friend to cheat off of their test or homework. As we shall see, different values, sometimes even good ones, come into conflict. Only when we bring Jesus and his values into our decision making will we have the moral clarity to make good decisions.

As is evident from the definition of core values, we cannot determine someone's core values, even our own, just by what the person says they are. Core values are determined by observing a person's *behavior.* Remember, core values are those values that cause us to make the decisions that we make, and the decisions that we make are reflected in our behavior.

I may think of myself as a loving, forgiving person, but if I am always highly critical of my wife and remember every slight or offense by her against me, I am deceiving myself. Although I may believe I am a loving, forgiving person, my actions belie my beliefs. I may think of myself as an honest person who can be relied upon to tell the truth at all times, but if I cheat on my income tax return my behavior says honesty is not a core value of mine; it is only a value I adhere to when it is convenient, or when I am afraid I might get caught.

Before you begin an in depth analysis of your own core values, however, I recommend that you begin with a less daunting task. I recommend that you begin with the exercises suggested below to help sensitize you to core values. The reason that I recommend that you not begin with your own core values is that it will be one of the more painful things that you will ever do, at least at times. One of the hardest things for any person to do is look at himself honestly and say to himself I am not living the values that I claim to believe in. The goal is to arrive at this point, but beginning there is like trying to run before we begin to walk.

To begin thinking about core values, pick a character or two from a favorite book, movie or television program, and analyze what that person's behavior reveals about his or her core values. Remember, core values can be good or bad; you should try to identify the good values and the bad values revealed by the character's actions. The character's behavior may show her to be loving, forgiving or generous, or it may show that she is full of anger, resentment and pride. Furthermore, try to determine whether the character is aware of what her true values are. As in real life, the character will often be unaware of what her behavior says about her true core values, or she doesn't care what her values are. As you do these exercises you will become more sensitive to core values and the relationship between core values and behavior.

You will also notice that in some popular movies, books or television programs the clever writing sometimes makes us oblivious to the appalling core values demonstrated by the characters. One such program was the popular long-running television series "Friends." With a name like that one expected the characters to demonstrate a strong sense of loyalty and trust to one another. Even the music in the program extolled friendship. But as often as not, the characters exhibited little loyalty to one another. They were more interested in going to bed with one another or a friend's boyfriend or girlfriend than they were in true loyalty or friendship. When you ask yourself what the character's behavior reveals about his or her core values, you may quickly conclude that this is someone you do not want to emulate.

Once you have used characters in movies, books and television programs to help you analyze core values, you are ready to move to the next step. Identify a friend or family member and analyze what that person's behavior reveals about his or her core values. A word of warning, however: *Do not, under any circumstances, share with the friend or family member what you believe about his or her core values, at least not if they are negative values.* The purpose of this exercise is not to have you sit in judgment of your friend or family member. The purpose is to get you focused on a person's core values and learn how you can recognize certain core values by a person's behavior. Observing a friend or family member's behavior to glean his core values is more personal than judging the core values of a character in a book or movie. It will help prepare you for the far more difficult and very personal task of evaluating your own behavior to determine what it reveals about your core values.

After a few weeks of observing the behavior of friends or family members to pinpoint their core values, you should be ready to evaluate your own behavior. I recommend that you do this during a regular devotion time, a time that includes prayer and devotional reading of scripture, as well as self-examination. In prayer, ask God to reveal what your behavior over the past day or two says about your *true* core values. If you ask earnestly and sincerely, and honestly reflect upon your behavior, your prayer will be answered. Over time, God will help you see yourself honestly. What you see at first may surprise you by how ugly it is, but do not beat yourself up. Ask God to forgive you and to help you change your behavior. As you pray and think about your behavior on a daily basis, using Jesus' values as a yardstick, you will find that the values that Jesus taught will gradually become your own core values. Remember, this is a process and you will not totally change over night. But you will definitely see a change in yourself over time.

As you continue this process of examining your behavior to determine whether your core values reflect what you profess to believe you will observe several things. You will notice that different core values sometimes come into conflict. The one that prevails is the one you hold most strongly. For example, the core value of being honest may come into conflict with the core value of being a loyal friend. If loyalty to friends prevails, you may become involved in cheating or in assisting your friend in covering up harmful or destructive behavior. How do you know which values should be the strongest? The values that Jesus taught are the ones that should take priority. As we shall see in future chapters, Jesus spoke directly to certain values that should be foremost in the life of his followers.

Another thing you will notice is that the default core value—the value that takes over if there is not a more strongly held value—is self-centeredness, or as I prefer to say, "I want what I want when I want it." As fallen and fallible human beings, this is a core value that we are born with, and it remains with us at varying strengths throughout the rest of our lives. In fact, as we look about us we see that self-centeredness is perhaps the strongest held value in our culture today. We want what we want when we want it, and that is the value that controls far too many of the decisions that we make.

The good news, however, is that core values can and do change over time. The Christian who wants to abide in Christ and have her faith inform all of her life, can, with God's help, learn to adopt and live by the values that Jesus taught. Those values, over time, will become core values to her and the decisions that she makes will increasingly be based on those core values. This process of developing core values that are consistent with the values that Jesus taught is nothing less than the development of Christian character. This process may be painful at times, but if you endure in pursuing the values that Jesus taught you will find that, as Paul said, "endurance produces character." (Romans 5:4)

Furthermore, this process of examining ourselves to see whether we are living the faith that we profess is not something that is optional; God expects it of us. In II Cor. 13:5 Paul instructs us to "Examine yourselves to see whether you are living in the faith. Test yourselves." He also commanded "Examine yourselves, and only then eat of the bread and drink of the cup." (I Cor. 11:28)

That is why part of our regular devotional time should include honestly examining our own behavior to see what it reveals about our core values. Be specific in examining your behavior and be brutally honest about what your behavior reveals about your true values. You cannot change (repent) until you acknowledge what your behavior reveals about what is at your core. Once you have acknowledged the bad values that your behavior reveals ask God to forgive you and to strengthen you to behave differently. Likewise, ask God to strengthen the good values that you see in your behavior. By asking God to help you change your core values to those of Jesus you are asking him to change your character to conform to the character of Jesus.

I also recommend that you keep a journal of your efforts to develop Christian core values. The written record will help focus your efforts and will also help you see the progress you will be making.

As explained more fully in future chapters, if you make a sincere effort to make Jesus' values your core values, you will observe a remarkable change in yourself over time. You simply cannot adopt the values that Jesus taught and allow them to seep into the core of your being without becoming a different person. Peter changed from an impetuous hothead to an apostle who urged followers of Jesus to discipline themselves and live holy lives (I Peter 1:13-16). John changed from a "Son of Thunder" (Mark 3:17) to the apostle of love (1 John 4:7-21).

By systematically examining your own behavior and asking God to strengthen within you the core values that Jesus taught you will appropriate for yourself God's promise given through the prophet Ezekiel:

> "A new heart I will give you, and a new spirit I will put within you; and I will remove from your body the heart of stone and give you a heart of flesh. I will put my spirit within you and make you follow my statutes and be careful to observe my ordinances." (Ezekiel 36:26-27).

## *QUESTIONS TO CONSIDER*

1. Are there decisions you have made in your life that you now regret? What caused you to make those decisions? Why do you now regret them?

2. Pick a character from one of your favorite books, movies or television programs. What are the core values of that character? What is it in his or her behavior that causes you to believe he or she has those core values?

3. Pick a friend or relative and identify one or two core values of that person. What is it in his or her behavior that causes you to believe he or she has those core values? (If the core values are negative, don't share them with your friend or relative, or with anyone else.)

4. What do you believe are some of your own core values? Do you believe that your behavior reflects those core values a) always; b) most of the time; or c) some of the time? What is the biggest hindrance to your living out your positive core values all the time?

5. How often do you stop and reflect on your own behavior and what your behavior says about your character and values? Are you willing to examine your own behavior on a regular basis to see what your behavior says your true core values are? Are you willing to ask God to help you do this and help you be honest with yourself?

6. Have you ever thought about what Jesus' core values were as demonstrated by his actions while he was here on earth? Try to identify two or three of Jesus' core values and explain how you came to that conclusion.

# CHAPTER 2

# WHAT JESUS HAD TO SAY ABOUT CORE VALUES

As discussed in the preceding chapter, although Jesus did not use the term "core values," his teaching always emphasized obedience to the Father through our actions. In the parable of the two sons (Matt. 21: 28-32) Jesus contrasted the actions of one son who promised to follow the instructions of his father to work in the vineyard, but did not, with the actions of the other son who told his father he would not work in the vineyard, but later changed his mind and did what he was told to do. Jesus was clearly unimpressed with the son who promised obedience, but failed to do what he promised. "Which of the two did the will of his father?" Jesus asked. (Matt. 21:31)

Moreover, Jesus was not hesitant to set the bar high for his followers. He instructed them to "Be perfect, therefore, as your heavenly Father is perfect." (Matt. 5:48) Obviously, Jesus knew that his disciples would never achieve perfection in this lifetime, but he wanted them to know that if they claimed his name he expected them to follow his example and his commandments as to how they should live their lives.

And Jesus left no room for doubt in his disciples that the example he set and the instructions he gave were directly from the Father—the God of Abraham, Isaac and Jacob. He told Philip "Whoever has seen me has seen the Father." (John 14:9) To the Pharisees he said "If you knew me, you would know my Father also," (John 8:19) and "the Son can do nothing on his own, but only what he sees the Father doing; for whatever the Father does, the Son does likewise." (John 5:19)

Even the most devout Christian can only imagine the intimate relationship between Jesus and the Father. Jesus perfectly abided in the Father, and therefore his decisions, his actions and his words were perfectly aligned with God's will. Likewise, Jesus wants his disciples (imperfect as we are) to abide in him so that we will bring our decisions, our actions and our words in line with the character and will of Jesus. We can only do that if we understand the values that Jesus taught and make them such a priority in our lives that they become our core values—the values that cause us to make the decisions we make.

Happily, Jesus provided an abundance of instruction on what our core values are to be. Although we find Jesus' teaching on how we are to live our lives throughout the gospels, nowhere is that teaching more concentrated or more direct than in the Sermon on the Mount (Matthew, chapters 5-7). Here, Jesus lays out for all who will listen a different way of life, a life lived in relationship with him and consistent with his values—so much so that Matthew tells us that those who were there were "astounded at his teaching." (Matt. 7:28) Perhaps they were astounded, at least in part, because they recognized that if they were to live as Jesus instructed their lives would be very different than the lives they were then living.

There are many points of view from which to approach the Sermon on the Mount. One can focus primarily on the theology inherent in Jesus statements. Some have focused on the social or the political ramifications of his teaching. Our focus, however, will be on the values that Jesus taught that will inform and direct our decisions and our behavior. Most of chapters 5-7 of Matthew deal expressly with our behavior and what is acceptable and what is unacceptable to God. Our goal is to learn to live our lives as Jesus taught, so that we may one day hear him say "Well done, good and trustworthy servant." (Matt: 25:21)

But it is not enough just to *learn* the values that Jesus taught. They must seep into our core so that we actually live out those values day by day. Accordingly, as you read each of the following chapters, examine yourself on how well you are living that core value. As you read another chapter, add it to the list of values by which you judge your own behavior. If you do this regularly and consistently you will become a different person; you will become the person God wants you to be, one who shares the same values that Jesus lived and taught.

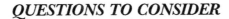

## *QUESTIONS TO CONSIDER*

1. Have you ever considered that your core values should be based upon your beliefs as a Christian? If not, where do most of your personal core values come from?

2. What are some of your favorite biblical stories? What were the core values of the people in those stories?

3. What are your favorite parables that Jesus taught? What values was Jesus emphasizing in these parables?

4. Were you surprised to read in this chapter that Jesus wants us to bring our decisions, our actions and our words in line with his character and will? What are the biggest obstacles in your life to your doing this? How will it affect your life if you do this?

# RECOGNIZE YOU ARE POOR IN SPIRIT

*"Blessed are the poor in spirit, for theirs is the kingdom of heaven."*
*(Matt. 5:3)*

This seems to be a strange place to begin a study of the development of core values to live by. Indeed, commentaries on the Sermon on the Mount have varied from extolling poverty to calling for social justice. But for one who is seeking to develop core values by which to live the Christian life, there is nowhere else to begin.

Jesus wants us to abide in him, to live a life in relationship with him that extends to all areas of our lives. But there is a major problem that inhibits that relationship. It is this: Jesus is without sin; we are not. There is a major flaw in us that causes us to miss the mark of what God intended for us (to miss the mark is the definition of sin).

Not only are we flawed, we are flawed to the extent we don't even recognize our flaw. The flaw is not that we do bad things. The flaw is that at the core of our being we ultimately listen to no voice but our own. We want what we want when we want it, and we don't much care what God or anyone else thinks about it. We are, as Isaiah said, "You who are wise in your own eyes, and shrewd in your own sight." (Is. 5:21) The flaw is our sinful nature which we have from birth. As David observed: "Indeed, I was born guilty, a sinner when my mother conceived me." (Ps. 51:5) Ours is a nature that is not just different from the nature of God; it is in direct opposition to him. If God wants one thing, we tend to want just the opposite—not in every decision we make, but in enough decisions that we are, as Paul describes, at enmity with God (Romans 3:9-18). Even when we decide to do what we think is right, we don't do it (Romans 7:14-20).

If we are in this condition, how can we ever live according to the values that Jesus taught—or even want to? The answer, of course, is that we cannot. An unrepentant sinner (one unwilling to change) cannot abide in Jesus because Jesus does not share our basic flaw—a sinful nature. Before we can enter into a relationship with God that will enable us to live as Jesus taught, there must be a breakthrough, a change from being the enemy of God to being in fellowship with him.

That breakthrough begins when we recognize the poverty of our spirit. We must come to recognize that we are not just separated from God but indifferent to him or consciously opposed to him. Although precisely how that comes about is beyond the scope of this book, it is important to understand that we don't come to this understanding on our own. Through the circumstances we find ourselves in as the result of our ignoring God in our decisions (as with the prodigal son, and as with Charles and Rachel), or by some other God-inspired method, we are confronted with the ugly fact that we are spiritually poor, living apart from God, with all the consequences that brings.

Although it may seem counter-intuitive, it is only when we recognize the poverty of our spirit that we first glimpse the possibility of another way of life—a life in the kingdom of heaven. That is a life in which we no longer live apart from or indifferent to God, but in harmony and fellowship with him. We receive forgiveness for ignoring or disobeying him; we want his values to become our values and his purposes to become our purposes. When we glimpse this other way of life we are ready to enter the kingdom of heaven.

As we shall see in the next chapter, this recognition of the poverty of our spirit—that we have a sinful nature that is opposed to God—will not

26

by itself bring us fully into the kingdom, but it is the first step on the road that leads into the kingdom, and that is why Jesus proclaims in the very first beatitude: "Blessed are the poor in spirit, for theirs is the kingdom of heaven."

This may seem to be merely a theological point, but it is much more. The recognition that we are all sinners—every one of us—is foundational to how we relate to God and to one another. In fact, as we come to understand that each of us is a sinner by nature in need of the grace and forgiveness of God, we quickly recognize that we are all in the same boat. You may be smarter, richer and more attractive than I am, but we both stand before God as sinners needing his grace and forgiveness. You may have accomplished much more in this life than I have but we are equal opportunity sinners. You have no reason to believe you are superior to me and I have no reason to believe I am superior to anyone else. Likewise, no racial or ethnic group stands in a favored position. We are all equal in our sinful nature before God.

If we make a commitment to Christ, accept his grace and forgiveness and commit to learning and living his values, we may sin less, but we must never forget that we still have a sinful nature that will promptly reassert itself the moment we cease to abide in him. That is why we must hold ourselves accountable daily.

The recognition that we have no grounds to feel superior to anyone else (even those who on the surface appear to be more proficient sinners than we are) will cause us to be less judgmental of others, less ready to find fault. As Jesus said, "First take the log out of your own eye, and then you will see clearly to take the speck out of your neighbor's eye." (Matt. 7:5) As we do this, the way we treat other people—even people we do not particularly like—will begin to change, and change profoundly. We begin to live in the kingdom of heaven.

Thus, the core value is:

*"I will always recognize that I am a sinner by nature in need of the grace and forgiveness of God—and so is everyone else."*

## QUESTIONS TO CONSIDER

1. Many people have difficulty thinking of themselves as sinners by nature. Is this a problem for you? What effect do you think it will have on you if you admit that you are poor in spirit?

2. Other people are so aware of their sinful nature or otherwise have such a low opinion of themselves that they feel unworthy and cannot imagine that they could ever find forgiveness from God. Is this a problem for you? Is it helpful to you to know that no one is worthy of God's grace and forgiveness, that we are all sinners in need of his mercy?

3. Have any of the circumstances of your life caused you to question whether you are living apart from or indifferent to God? What were the circumstances and what brought them about? What conclusions did you reach about your relationship to God and what impact did that have on your life?

4. If you have already begun to recognize the poverty of your spirit and realize that you need the grace and forgiveness of God, how did you come to that point? How has it affected how you make decisions and how you live your life?

5. If you have already begun to recognize the poverty of your spirit, what effect did that have on your relationships with other people? With how you view other people?

# CHAPTER 4

# BE WILLING TO CHANGE

*"Blessed are those who mourn, for they will be comforted."* (Matt. 5:4)

As with the first beatitude, this one seems contradictory. How can anyone find comfort through mourning? The answer is that Jesus is not referring to weeping over our sins; he is referring to regretting our sins to the point we are willing to change.

In the first beatitude Jesus says we are blessed if we recognize that we are spiritually poor. But we cannot remain there. After glimpsing that there is another way of life, we must proceed on to enter into that new way of life. We must change from a person whose chief core value is "I want what I want when I want it" to a person who seeks to have her character molded by the values of Jesus. This change is such a profound one that Jesus likens it to being "born again." (John 3: 2-8) Paul said that "if anyone is in Christ, there is a new creation: everything old has passed away; see, everything has become new." (II Cor. 5:17) Clearly, this is much more than just a change of attitude; it is a change of who we are at the core of our being.

The biblical term for this change is repentance. To repent literally means to go in a different direction. It means that we change from someone who is indifferent or even antagonistic to God to one who is obedient to God, one who is willing to acknowledge his sins and return to God whenever he may wander. This was not a peripheral issue with

Jesus. Matthew tells us that Jesus began his ministry by proclaiming "Repent, for the kingdom of heaven has come near." (Matt. 4:17)

If this requirement to repent—to change, to become more "Christ like"—is so important why are we so reluctant to do it? Part of the reason is that we badly underestimate the strength of the core values that we have developed over a lifetime of self-centered living. After wanting what we want when we want it for most of our lives, we will not easily give up our self-centeredness, even if we have glimpsed a new way of life in harmony with God rather than apart from or indifferent to God. Jesus readily acknowledged how difficult this profound change would be. He said "If any want to become my followers, let them deny themselves (i.e., no longer live a self-centered life) and take up their cross and follow me." (Matt. 16:24)

Jesus also knew that this would be a painful process for us at times. Although mourning or crying over our sins is not required for repentance, mourning does often accompany repentance. We don't change easily or painlessly, even when we deplore what we have done or despise what we have become. Charles knew that cheating and padding his expense account was wrong, and had guilt pangs about it, but he never repented. He could have told his employer at an earlier date of the small amounts he had wrongfully taken and perhaps found forgiveness. By his unwillingness to change and adhere to the values he knew to be right, he sank ever deeper into a pattern of living that could devastate his life, and eventually did so. He simply was unwilling to repent—to change—while there was still time.

Rachel was unwilling to repent after moving in with Roger, which she knew to be wrong. She was still unwilling to repent even after her relationship with Roger came to an unhappy ending. The result was that she repeated her error and entered into another similar relationship with Steve. It also, predictably, came to an unhappy conclusion. At her core, Rachel believed that happiness, security and self-fulfillment would come through a relationship with a man she loved—even one who had made no commitment to her—rather than through a relationship with God, who loved her unconditionally and who desired an eternal relationship with her.

The irony with both Charles and Rachel is that because they were unwilling to go through the pain of repentance when they first began to get off track, the pain they ultimately suffered was far greater. They, like many, only began to see the need for change when the pain became almost unbearable.

Clearly, repenting is one of the most difficult things we are called upon to do. And that is why it is so important to recognize the promise that Jesus made to those who are willing to repent. He promised his disciples that they would be comforted. On the night before Jesus was crucified he promised his disciples that he would send the Holy Spirit to them and they would have peace (John 14: 15-27); in other words, they would be comforted by the Holy Spirit. Thus, though the process of repentance may be painful, Jesus promised that if we come to the point of repentance we will eventually be comforted by God the Holy Spirit.

This process of repenting each time we sin is fundamental to the Christian life. On the day of Pentecost those present heard Peter explain the astonishing events they had just seen. They asked "What should we do?" Peter's response began with the need for repentance:

> "Repent, and be baptized everyone of you in the name of Jesus Christ so that your sins may be forgiven; and you will receive the gift of the Holy Spirit. For the promise is for you, for your children, and for all who are far away, everyone whom the Lord our God calls to him." (Acts 2:37-39).

The Apostle John, in his first letter to the early church, likewise emphasized the need for confession of sins and repentance, and acknowledged that we are all sinners in need of repentance:

> "If we say that we have no sin, we deceive ourselves, and the truth is not in us. If we confess our sins, he who is faithful and

just will forgive us our sins and cleanse us from all unrighteous-
ness." (I John 1:8-9)

We must keep short accounts with God by repenting daily.
Therefore, the core value is:

*"When confronted with my own sin, I will acknowledge it, seek forgiveness
and commit to change, with God's help."*

## *QUESTIONS TO CONSIDER*

1.  What do you think of when you hear the word repentance? Do you
    think of sincere regret, perhaps to the point of crying? Do you think
    that a person can regret and cry but still not change, i.e., repent?
    Has this ever happened to you?

2.  What is the biggest impediment to your repenting, to changing
    some aspect of your life or your character? How strong is the core
    value in you "I want what I want when I want it"? What tangible steps
    can you take to overcome this impediment?

3.  Pain is often a part of repentance because it is often quite difficult
    for us to change. We often don't want to give up our sins. Have you
    experienced pain as part of repentance? Was the result of your
    repentance worth the pain you endured?

4.  Jesus promised that those who repent will be comforted. Have you
    experienced this comfort? Please explain.

# CHAPTER 5

# THE MEEK SHALL INHERIT THE EARTH

*"Blessed are the meek, for they will inherit the earth."* *(Matt. 5:5)*

If the first two beatitudes are difficult for us, this one is more so. When we hear the word "meek," we usually think of someone who is a milquetoast, or a doormat, someone whom we may pity, but never imitate. Who really wants to be called "meek?"

In the gospel accounts of Jesus' ministry he hardly fits the mold of one we think of as meek or humble. Upon his triumphal entry to Jerusalem on Palm Sunday, he went to the temple " . . . and drove out all who were selling and buying in the temple, and he overturned the tables of the money changers and the seats of those who sold doves." He even told the leaders of the temple "You are making it (the temple) a den of robbers." (Matt. 21: 12-13). And in full public view, with his disciples and crowds surrounding him, he denounced the leading figures of the day—the scribes and Pharisees—in language so strong that even a modern day politician or pundit would be reluctant to use it (see Matt. 23: 1-36): "You snakes, you brood of vipers! How can you escape being sentenced to hell?" (Matt. 23: 33)

One of the primary characteristics of Jesus during his earthly ministry is that he was always strong. He faced constant adversity from the chief priests, scribes and Pharisees; he was doubted by his own disciples at times, and, indeed, betrayed by one of them. He dealt with fickle crowds and even his own family wondered about him. "Prophets are not without honor, except in their hometown, and among their own kin, and in their own house" was how Jesus described his own situation (Mark 6: 4). Yet Jesus was steadfast in fulfilling the mission that he had been given, even to the point of death. How could one so strong and so steadfast ever be accused of being meek or humble? Nothing distracted him from his mission.

And yet this is what Jesus said of himself: "Take my yoke upon you, and learn from me; for I am gentle and humble in heart, and you will find rest for your souls." (Matt. 11: 29). Clearly, Jesus did not believe that being strong and steadfast were inconsistent with being gentle and humble in heart. The reason that we have difficulty reconciling these two characteristics of Jesus is that in our view of the world it is not the meek but the strong and powerful that win. The leaders of industry, government, business, entertainment, and academia expect, and usually receive, deference and privilege. Although we give lip service to the importance of humility, few truly make humility one of their core values. Perhaps we are afraid that if we appear to be humble we cannot also appear to be strong.

This, however, was not an issue for Jesus. In fact, on the final night before his death he dramatically demonstrated how his disciples, whom he knew would be the leaders of the church, should exercise their leadership. Jesus stripped off his outer robe, put a towel around himself, as a common servant would, and began washing the feet of some very astonished disciples. Peter even asked him incredulously "Lord, are you going to wash my feet?" (John 13:6) And, of course, he was. Once Jesus had finished this act of a servant he made it unmistakably clear to them what he had done. "You call me Teacher and Lord—and you are right, for that is what I am. So if I, your Lord and Teacher, have washed your feet, you also ought to wash one another's feet. For I have set you an example, that you also should do as I have done to you." (John 13: 13-15)

So, the strength required for leadership in the church would go hand in hand with the humility of a servant, one who was willing to take on the most menial of tasks regardless of his "position." Paul also referred to the "meekness and gentleness of Christ." (II Cor. 10: 1)

Why is it so important that we, as followers of Christ, develop the core value of humility, or meekness? Why does Jesus address humility immediately after repentance and before mercy, purity of heart and peacemaking? It is because humility is the cure for pride. Pride involves having an inordinately high or unjustified opinion of one's self. It involves believing that we are better than other people, or that we stand in a favored position with God due to our own goodness or merit. Scripture uniformly warns against pride. "When pride comes, then comes disgrace." (Prov. 11:2) "Pride goes before destruction, and a haughty spirit before a fall." (Prov. 16:18) Jesus identified pride as one of the evils that comes from within and defiles a person. (Mark 7:22) One cannot simultaneously be humble and full of pride. If Jesus considered himself to be "gentle and humble in heart" how much more so should we be humble. If we truly understand that we are "poor in spirit" we will also understand that we have good reason to be humble.

Our problem, however, is not so much in being humble before God, but in being humble in our relationships with other people. We readily admit in our prayers that we are sinners, but if a friend or acquaintance points out our sin to us, we are usually offended. We may even accuse the friend of being judgmental. Why this inconsistency? It is usually because we have not truly learned what it means to be humble or meek. We still want what we want, and what we do *not* want is for someone else, even a friend (or especially a friend), to tell us how we have missed the mark, even if that is precisely what we need to be told.

If we are truly humble we will always treat others with dignity and respect, even if we strenuously disagree with that person and even if that person holds views that we abhor. Any time we find ourselves looking down on another person, regardless of the reason, we should be aware that humility has left us. We may be thankful that we are not in the same situation as someone less fortunate, or that we do not hold the same views as that person, but we must always remember that it is only by the grace of God that we are not in similar circumstances.

Finally, as we shall see again in chapter 11, there is significance to the order in which Jesus presented the Sermon on the Mount. The admonition in this beatitude to be meek or humble in heart comes immediately after the admonition to repent and immediately before the admonition to hunger and thirst for righteousness. If we earnestly seek to repent of our sins and earnestly hunger and thirst for righteousness, the admonition by Jesus to be humble will tend to take care of itself.

As with the other beatitudes, this one comes with a promise. If we are truly meek we will inherit the earth. We will be confident that we are living within the will of God, or at least earnestly trying to do so, with God's help. Jesus promised that those who earnestly follow him will "receive a hundred fold now in this age . . . and in the age to come eternal life." (Mark 10: 29-31). This does not mean that we will have everything that we ever want in this life, but we will be in the proper relationship—one characterized by humility—with both God and man.

Therefore, the core value is:

*"I will never consider myself to be better than any other person, and will treat every person with dignity and respect."*

## QUESTIONS TO CONSIDER

1.  What do you think of when you hear the word "meek" or the word "humble"? Are these characteristics that you have aspired to?

2. Do you think that most people believe one who is meek or humble can also be strong and powerful? Do you personally believe this?

3. What do you believe are the keys to being truly humble or meek? What does it take in terms of behavior and attitude? Do you see any relationship between being meek and humble, and recognizing the poverty of our spirit?

4. Do you have difficulty treating another person with dignity and respect when you strongly disagree with that person on some significant issue, such as a political issue, or some religious or moral issue? What do you think you should do about this?

5. How do you usually respond to criticism from other people? How do you feel about friends or relatives pointing out character flaws or some sinful area of your life? How do you think you should respond to such statements in light of Jesus' admonition to be meek or humble?

# CHAPTER 6

# OUR FIRST PRIORITY

*"Blessed are those who hunger and thirst for righteousness, for they will be filled." (Matt. 5:6)*

This beatitude is one that has lost some of its impact because most of us know little of true hunger or true thirst. In our affluence we seldom face hunger or thirst in the same sense used in the original Greek in which the New Testament was written. The words used refer to one close to starvation or close to dying for lack of water. Given the conditions in the time Jesus spoke these words, those listening would understand what true hunger and true thirst were. Many of them had experienced true hunger or true thirst, or both, and knew they would likely experience them again. One of the best biblical examples is Esau who was so famished upon returning from the field that he sold his birthright to his brother Jacob for a bowl of lentil stew! (Gen. 25:29-34)

But why is Jesus saying that one who hungers or thirsts *for righteousness* in this way will be blessed? What is it about nearly dying for something, even righteousness, that would cause Jesus to say "they will be filled?" One who has experienced true hunger or true thirst would understand. A person who is truly hungry or truly thirsty can think of almost nothing else except getting food or water. Other things that normally occupy our thoughts are simply shoved to the background of our minds, only to resurface when these basic needs are met. One who has wandered in the desert without water, whose body is dehydrated and whose lips are dry, cracked and bleeding, will have no internal arguments over his priorities in life. It is simple; he has one priority: get water or die. Everything else becomes secondary.

As he often did, Jesus used vivid imagery to make his point: seeking righteousness must take first priority in our lives. The righteousness he refers to is being in a right relationship with him and also with other people. In chapter 1, we discussed how Jesus wants us to abide in him. That includes submitting our decisions, our actions and, yes, our priorities to him. Unless we give this our first priority in life, we will never truly be able to abide in him. We will just visit with him from time to time. Jesus is not seeking occasional visitors; he wants disciples who are sold out to him.

This notion of giving God first priority in everything we do or say is not an easy thing for us to accept, particularly in modern western culture. We take pride in our independence, and we are reluctant to commit totally to anything, even ideas or people we agree with. We view it as confining, and perhaps bordering on extremism. After all, most of the people that seem to be so totally committed are involved in some type of cult, or are engaged in some other type of extreme behavior. How do we distinguish what Jesus is asking of us from the extremism of those who represent everything that we deplore?

The most important distinction is that Jesus is telling us to give first priority to our relationship with God, and consequently with him as the Son of God. This total commitment to Jesus is not meant to oppress or confine us; it is intended to liberate us. In the sixth chapter of Matthew (also part of the Sermon on the Mount) Jesus addresses a very modern problem: worry. Although the Jews of that day had more to worry about than we do today, we match them worry for worry. As I write this chapter we are in one of the worse financial crises the world has experienced in over 50 years. Many people are worried sick. Nevertheless, we remain at least as well off as those who listened to Jesus' words on the mount.

They worried whether they would have food to eat, water to drink and clothes to wear. But Jesus addressed their concerns by telling them that, as important as those things are, giving first priority to our relationship with God is even more important. Listen to Jesus' comforting words to them to allay their fears and worries:

> "Therefore do not worry, saying, 'What will we eat?' or 'What will we drink?' or 'What will we wear?' For it is the Gentiles who strive for all these things; and indeed your heavenly Father knows that you need all these things. But strive first for the kingdom of God and his righteousness, and all these things will be given to you as well." (Matt. 6:31-33)

When we consider these words of Jesus, and take them seriously, we realize it is an amazing, even radical, statement Jesus is making: if we give first priority to our relationship with him—if we truly seek to abide in him—there will be no need to worry about those things that we so often worry about. Our needs will be met. This is not an endorsement of socialism or any other political or economic system, nor is it a promise that we won't have to work to earn a living. It is a simple affirmation of the statement that King David made: "The Lord is my shepherd, I shall not want." (Psalm 23:1)

Although Charles had attended church and felt that he was called to become a CPA, along the way he failed to give God first priority in his life. He decided that he would provide for his family in his own way even if it meant embezzling money from his employer. He was willing to trade his integrity for the money he could steal from those who entrusted him with the finances of his company.

Rachel failed to give her relationship with God first priority in her life. As many do, she made the decision to put a romantic relationship at the top of her priority list, and it led her into heartache and regret, not once but twice.

If Charles had taken seriously Jesus' words to seek first the kingdom of God and his righteousness and made it a core value, he would have avoided getting so badly off track. He could have lived more modestly, or perhaps even found more success in his company without having to resort to embezzlement. If Rachel had sought first a right relationship with God, she would have been more discerning in her relationships with men. She would have waited for a man who had similar values and who would have been willing to make a commitment to her in marriage. They both set their own priorities and those priorities led them to a place they never thought they would be. Their lives became the result of the decisions they made based upon their own priorities, not the priorities of one hungering and thirsting for righteousness.

The examples of Charles and Rachel may seem too difficult for you to relate to. You may be wondering if I am suggesting that you must be perfect in your relationship with God to avoid problems of the types that they faced. If that is your fear, be reassured. God certainly knows that you will not live a perfect life. Jesus did not say that it is those who have a perfect relationship with God that will be blessed. It is those who hunger and thirst after righteousness that will be blessed. In other words, it is those that make their relationship with God their first priority that will be blessed. Jesus was a realist when it came to human nature. He knows you far better than you know yourself; he certainly does not expect perfection. But he does expect you, as one who claims the name of "Christian," to put your relationship with him first in your life.

Furthermore, he promises that if you put him first you will be filled. What is better than the first drink of water when one is truly thirsty, or the first bite of food when one is truly hungry? You are filled with that which you want the most. Likewise, Jesus promises that if you hunger and thirst for your relationship with him, you will be filled with his presence in your life. God will no longer seem to be distant or unapproachable but a welcoming presence whom you know intimately and who knows you intimately. As David, one who made his relationship with God his first priority for most of his life, said: "Even before a word is on my tongue, O Lord, you know it completely." (Ps. 139:4) That is intimate knowledge.

Imagine living like this. It will truly be a new life. To help make it so, the core value is:

*"I will at all times give my relationship with God first priority in my life."*

## QUESTIONS TO CONSIDER

1. What is your reaction to the idea that God wants us to give him first priority in all aspects of our lives, in all that we do or say? Is that something that you want to do, or do you view this as a duty that you will try to perform?

2. Most of us do not have a problem with giving God first priority in some areas of our lives, but we prefer to set our own priorities in other areas of our lives. Is this true of you? In what areas of your life are you reluctant to allow God to have first priority?

3. Is worry a problem for you? Do you believe that you worry too much? What is it that you worry about the most? Are the areas of your life in which you are reluctant to give God first priority also the areas of your life about which you worry the most?

4. In the stories of Charles and Rachel given in the first chapter, where did they fail to give God first priority in their lives? What was the result? If you had been a close friend of Charles or Rachel, what advice would you have given them? How would you go about giving them that advice?

5. Jesus promised that if we give God first priority in our lives we will be filled with his presence in our lives. What do you imagine your life would be like if you gave God first priority in all areas of your life? How do you think God's presence in your life would manifest itself?

# CHAPTER 7

# THE MERCIFUL SHALL RECEIVE MERCY

*"Blessed are the merciful, for they will be shown mercy." (Matt. 5:7)*

If there is any trait that characterized Jesus' ministry on earth, it was that he was merciful, or compassionate. Indeed the purpose of his coming to earth was to bring God's mercy to sinners (which includes everyone of us). This is the good news that Jesus proclaimed. To Nicodemus, the Pharisee who came to Jesus by night to inquire about his ministry and his message, Jesus laid it out plainly:

"For God so loved the world that he gave his only Son, so that everyone who believes in him may not perish but may have eternal life. Indeed, God did not send the Son into the world to condemn the world, but in order that the world might be saved through him." (John 3:16-17)

The message of God being merciful and expecting his children to be merciful was not a new message with Jesus; Jesus was just the person-ification of mercy. David proclaimed the mercy of God, saying that God "crowns you with steadfast love and mercy . . ." (Ps. 103:4) And again: "But you, O Lord, are a God merciful and gracious, slow to anger and abounding in steadfast love and faithfulness." (Ps. 86:15) The prophet Jonah, who wanted revenge on the people of Nineveh, explained to God that he fled to Tarshish to avoid doing what God had commanded him to do (proclaim to the people of Nineveh that they must repent or be destroyed) because "I knew that you are a gracious God and merciful, slow to anger, and abounding in steadfast love, and ready to relent from punishing." (Jonah 4:2)

Although the message of God being merciful may not have been new with Jesus, he demonstrated it in unforgettable ways. One day when Jesus was teaching at the temple, the Pharisees brought before him a woman who had been caught in the very act of adultery. They asked Jesus whether the penalty prescribed in the law of Moses— stoning—should be carried out. The woman clearly was guilty, and the law was the law, but Jesus responded simply: "Let anyone among you who is without sin be the first to throw a stone at her." (John 8:7) Note that Jesus did not say what she had done was not wrong; he simply refused to condemn her. "Neither do I condemn you. Go your way, *and from now on do not sin again.*" (John 8:11)

On another occasion, Jesus was passing through Samaria on the way to Jerusalem. Ten lepers approached him seeking mercy from him, namely healing. It is important to note that to the Jews and the Samaritans alike lepers were the dregs of society. They had to shout out as they approached anyone "leper, leper" to avoid anyone coming into contact with them and possibly contracting the disease. They were the lowest of the low and yet Jesus had mercy on them. He instructed them to go show themselves to the priests, and as they went they were healed of their leprosy. (Luke 17:11-19) Only one of the ten returned to thank Jesus, and he was a Samaritan, whom Jews disdained. But Jesus was impressed by the man's response to the mercy he had been shown. He told him "your faith has made you well." (Luke 17:19)

Although we know mercy or compassion when we see it or experience it, having a working definition will be helpful to develop this core value within us. To be merciful is to show compassion; it is refraining from the infliction of suffering by one who has the right or power to inflict it. It is also removing or reducing suffering by one who has the power or ability to remove or reduce suffering. Note that although the previous beatitudes focus on what is going on inside us (recognizing the poverty of our spirit, being willing to repent, giving God first priority in our life) this beatitude focuses on our outward response to others. They will bear the result of our decision to show compassion or withhold it.

To the woman caught in adultery, Jesus showed mercy by refusing to join those who wished to subject her to the most severe punishment that could be imposed for her sin. Had Jesus insisted that the law of Moses be enforced, the Pharisees undoubtedly would have carried out the punishment. To the leper, on the other hand, Jesus showed mercy by exercising his power of healing to reduce the man's suffering.

In his parables, Jesus clearly demonstrated the extent to which God would go to show compassion to his children. In the parable of the prodigal son (Luke 15:11-32), Jesus described a father whose compassion knew no bounds. The prodigal son treated his father with contempt, demanded his inheritance as though the father was already dead, and only repented when his money was gone and he had nowhere else to turn. This story easily could have been used to show the folly of a young, disobedient son, but that is not the point that Jesus made. The point Jesus made was that our Father is compassionate beyond anything we can imagine. When the older brother failed to show compassion for his younger brother, he received a mild rebuke from the father, who was grieved by his older son's lack of compassion.

Many other scriptures could be cited to demonstrate Jesus showing mercy or compassion on those who were undeserving or merely unfortunate, such as the leper. But what is the point of this beatitude? It is, of course, to encourage us to show compassion; Jesus says that we will be blessed if we are merciful. The point Jesus is making, however, goes beyond that. He says that *if* we are merciful, we will be shown mercy. The corollary of this is that if we are not merciful we have no right to expect to receive mercy. As we will see in chapter 18, there is a parallel to this when Jesus addresses the forgiveness of our sins. He says that if we do not forgive others their sins against us, God will not forgive us our sins. That is a frightening thought. Yet every time we say the Lord's prayer, we pray, usually without much thought to what we are actually asking of God: "Forgive us our sins, *as we forgive those who sin against us.*"

Jesus' teaching about mercy carries the same idea. In fact, forgiving those who sin against us is closely connected with showing compassion. He expects us to be compassionate people; if we are not, we will likely not receive compassion. Jesus well knew that we are not nearly as ready to show mercy or compassion as we are to receive it, but that is what he calls upon us to do. We must make it a core value and examine ourselves daily to insure we are living out Jesus' command to be merciful.

Again, it is in our nature—our sinful nature—to be self focused and to seek what we want rather than to show compassion. Part of living in the kingdom of heaven—a very important part—is to show compassion for others. Even those who do not live in the kingdom of heaven will recognize that we are compassionate when we follow Jesus' example. It is worth noting that in the early days of the church, as it spread into the broader culture, it was not primarily the theology that initially attracted people to the Christian faith; it was the love and compassion that they showed to one another. Everyone can recognize compassion (and everyone wants it) even if he or she is not ready to give it. But as they see us being compassionate people they will be encouraged to be compassionate also. If we, as Christians, make compassion a core value so that our lives reflect the compassionate nature of the one we worship, we will attract those who know us to the kingdom of God, and compassion will become more common than it now is.

The core value is:

*"I will always show mercy (compassion) to others and encourage others to do likewise."*

## *QUESTIONS TO CONSIDER*

1.  Read again the definition of mercy in this chapter and think of ways that you can show mercy or compassion each day. Give some examples. What is holding you back?

2.  In the parable of the prodigal son (Matt. 15: 11-32) who do you relate to the most, the father, the prodigal son or the older brother? Why? Can you relate to the older brother? Why or why not?

3.  What do you think about Jesus' statement that it is the merciful that will receive mercy? Have you experienced times in your life that you received mercy or compassion even when you were not being merciful or compassionate yourself? If so, how did you feel about the person showing compassion although he or she was not receiving mercy or compassion?

4.  What relationship have you observed between anger and compassion? Have there been instances in your life in which you have been able to be compassionate while being angry with the person to whom you have shown compassion? Was it more difficult while you were angry?

5.  What do you believe you need to do to make showing mercy and compassion a core value of yours?

# THE PURE IN HEART
# WILL SEE GOD

*"Blessed are the pure in heart, for they will see God." (Matt. 5:8)*

This is perhaps the most difficult of the beatitudes for us to relate to. Who really sees himself as pure in heart? Who truly believes that we can ever become pure in heart? For most of us, we can more readily identify with the "poor in spirit" than we can with the "pure in heart." Speaking for myself, even on those occasions when I am pretty sure that I am being obedient to God, I do not see myself as being pure in heart. I know myself too well to think that my heart is pure. But this beatitude cannot be avoided. Jesus says that if I want to see God I must become pure in heart.

Jesus was not the first to make such a statement. David proclaimed:

Who shall ascend the hill of the Lord?
   And who shall stand in his holy place?
Those who have clean hands and pure hearts,
   who do not lift up their souls to what is false,
and do not swear deceitfully.
(Psalm 24:3-4)

In fact, David even invited God to examine his heart to see if it was pure.

Search me, O God, and know my heart;
   test me and know my thoughts.
See if there is any wicked way in me,
   and lead me in the way everlasting.
(Psalm 139:23-24)

Was David so certain of his own goodness and righteousness that he believed his heart was perfectly pure? Hardly. The same man who wrote the passages above also acknowledged before God:

For I know my transgressions,
   and my sin is ever before me.
Against you, you alone, have I sinned,
   and done what is evil in your sight,
So that you are justified in your sentence
   and blameless when you pass judgment.
Indeed, I was born guilty,
   a sinner when my mother conceived me.
(Psalm 51:3-5)

This was no false modesty on the part of David. For the full story of how far David fell, read II Samuel, chapters 11 and 12. He was guilty of lust, adultery, deceit and murder, not to mention a complete abuse of his power as king. Given how greatly God had blessed David previously it was a mystifying moral failure on the part of one who clearly knew better. If the same man who wrote the most beautiful and faith inspiring psalms, such as Psalm 23 and Psalm 103, can fall so far, what chance do we have of ever being pure in heart? And how could David ever be described as "a man after his (God's) own heart?" (I Sam. 13:14)

Actually, David, among all biblical characters, helps us understand what it means to be pure of heart. The problem is that sin clouds our moral vision. When we allow sin to enter into us (and it always comes invited, not against our will) we can no longer see clearly the road that God wants us to travel. It lures us to deviate onto a side road that will never get us to our intended destination unless we turn around and go back to the road that God has for us. Sin prevents us from seeing God as he is and ourselves as we are. As Proverbs tells us "All one's ways may be pure in one's own eyes, but the Lord weighs the spirit." (Prov.16:2)

Once David allowed himself to lust after Bathsheba his moral vision was clouded and he promptly forgot the core values that had brought him from a simple shepherd boy to the king of a united Israel, blessed by God more than David or his subjects ever imagined. But with a clouded moral vision his pure heart became anything but pure, and he committed in short order a series of sins that are still shocking to read about.

How, then, can David be an example of one who was pure of heart? It is because being pure in heart does not mean that we live in sinless perfection. Other than Jesus himself, none of us will ever be free of sin at all times. None of us can expect to live sin-free lives despite our best efforts ("all have sinned." Rom. 3:23). What God expects of the pure in heart is not perfection but a willingness to seek to keep ourselves free from sin, and to promptly acknowledge our sins when we do sin. This is the basis of David's purity of heart. In a time when a man could lose his life for even suggesting that a Mid-Eastern king was wrong, Nathan confronted David with his sin, and David humbly accepted Nathan's rebuke. Listen to David's contrition and his desire to once again be intimate with the Lord:

> Purge me with hyssop, and I shall be clean;
>    wash me, and I shall be whiter than snow.
> Let me hear joy and gladness;
>    let the bones that you have crushed rejoice.
> Hide your face from my sins,
>    and blot out all my iniquities.
> Create in me a clean heart, O God,
>    and put a new and right spirit within me.
> Do not cast me away from your presence,
>    and do not take your holy spirit from me.
> Restore to me the joy of your salvation,
>    and sustain in me a willing spirit.
> (Ps. 51:7-12)

That is true repentance, and it was typical of David; when he erred he always repented promptly. (For another episode of David sinning, see II Sam. 24:1-25) Hopefully, our sins won't be as dramatic as David's were but we should always be as quick to acknowledge our sin and to repent. The key to our becoming pure in heart is to quickly acknowledge our sin, change our behavior (repent) and earnestly try to avoid that sin in the future, with God's help.

But it is not just the sins of the flesh that we must avoid (or promptly repent of) if we are to be pure in heart. As we shall see in Chapter 11, one of the biggest impediments to our being pure in heart is anger. We simply cannot be pure of heart while we hold on to our anger. We all have flashes of anger, some justified and some not, but we are never supposed to hold on to that anger. Anger that is retained eventually leads to bitterness, and can be with us for years, interfering with or destroying our relationships with others, even family members.

Anger and bitterness interfere with our ability to see God and his will for our lives. Anger and bitterness also interfere with our becoming loving, compassionate people. God intends for each of us to develop into the person he wants us to be, a unique person with a pure and loving spirit. We simply cannot become that person while we hold on to our anger. Most angry or bitter people act pretty much alike (that's how we recognize that they are angry or bitter), but love can show itself in a variety of ways. If you want to be the unique person that you were meant to be you must develop a pure heart, and anger and bitterness have no place in a pure heart.

The sins of the flesh begin with something interfering with the purity of our heart, such as our own lust. That may lead to outward actions, as with David, that take us far from God. Likewise, the sins of the heart, such as anger, also come about when we let our own self-centeredness lead to anger. We want what we want when we want it, and when we don't get it, anger often rushes in. The first casualty is the purity of our heart. Unless we promptly repent, we will no longer "see God" as Jesus promised.

Finally, we must recognize that if we are to become pure in heart we must get control over our thought life as well as our actions. In chapter 1, we said that we can determine someone's core values by his or her behavior. That is true, but it is also true that most of our behavior is preceded by our thoughts. We must never assume that we can live an inward thought life that is at odds with the core values that Jesus taught without that inward thought life affecting our core values and consequently our behavior. As Proverbs admonishes us: "Keep your heart with all vigilance, for from it flow the springs of life." (Prov. 4:23) If we want the springs of life flowing from our heart to be pure, we must monitor our thought life to keep out the impurities.

Again, none of us will be perfectly pure in heart in this lifetime, but by seeking to be pure in heart—and promptly seeking forgiveness when we are not—we will begin to "see God" (and God's will for our life) as Jesus promised.

The core value is:

*"I will always seek to be pure in heart and will promptly seek forgiveness when my thoughts or actions are not pure."*

## QUESTIONS TO CONSIDER

1. Does it seem inconsistent to you that a person can be "poor in spirit" and "pure in heart" at the same time? Based on this chapter how do you explain that?

2. Which of the psalms written by David are your favorites? Do you have difficulty understanding how the same person who wrote these psalms also committed the acts described in II Samuel, chapters 11

and 12? Do you have difficulty thinking of yourself as being pure in heart because of some of the things that you have done?

3. Do you agree with the statement in this chapter that "Sin prevents us from seeing God as he is and ourselves as we are?" If so, how can this understanding help you in your prayers? Is asking God to allow us to see ourselves honestly something that we should be praying for?

4. Among biblical characters David was willing to admit his own sin better than most. Among the core values that we have studied so far, which one do you think most helped David be ready to admit his own sin? Read Psalm 51 to help you answer this question.

5. Which creates the bigger problem for you in attempting to be pure of heart, the sins of the flesh or the sins of the heart? Regardless of which is the bigger problem, how do you plan to deal with it?

6. Have anger and bitterness caused you to be less willing to forgive or to seek forgiveness? Do you believe that you should deal with your anger and bitterness to help you become and remain pure in heart? Do you see the importance of speaking to God daily in prayer to help you overcome anger and bitterness?

# BE A PEACEMAKER

*"Blessed are the peacemakers for they will be called sons of God."*
*(Matt. 5:9)*

In the beginning there was no need for peacemaking. God created a world that he declared was good, and with which he was pleased. After he created man and woman they lived in harmony with God. But that did not last long. Adam and Eve disobeyed God, as all of us have since, and there was a separation between God and man that has continued to this day. The story of the Bible after the third chapter of Genesis is about God's efforts to reconcile himself—to make peace—with mankind. That has been the primary work of God in this world since then, as Jesus made clear in the third chapter of the Gospel of John. Likewise, he expects those of us who have made a commitment to him to make peace with one another. It is the work of "sons of God."

If there is anything that this world needs it is more peacemaking. On an international level, lasting peace is an elusive goal. More people died in wars during the 20th century than perhaps in the entire history of mankind. The current century has not yet shown the promise of significant improvement. On the personal level, we all want peace in our lives rather than arguments, disputes and broken relationships. But, sadly, those who claim the name of Christ frequently do little better in their relationships than those who openly reject or ignore Christ.

That is even true in the most intimate of relationships—marriage. Christian marriages end in divorce about as frequently as those which are not Christian. Clearly, we need to make peacemaking one of our core values if we are to be obedient to Jesus, and if we expect to have peace in our own lives.

Fortunately, Jesus did not just tell us to be peacemakers; he also gave instructions on how to do it. In Matt. 5:38-48, which we will address in more detail in chapters 14 and 15, Jesus tells us to avoid retaliation and to love our enemies. These two things are easy to say but difficult to do; yet if we conscientiously try to do them we will find that peace is the fruit of our efforts.

The problem with retaliation begins early in life. The baby brother takes the sister's doll and she bops him on the head. Once we learn that taking other people's things is wrong and that bopping the wrongdoer on the head is not the proper solution, we begin to use other means: insults, slurs, gossip, slights and hateful statements. Sometimes these things are done in jest (although a lot of what we really intend to say is said in jest), but the damage done is often the same, and leads to broken relationships. These things are going to happen in life and they are going to happen long before one is an adult. As a Christian, how do we deal with them?

Jesus' instruction is to avoid retaliation. The normal course of events is that you make a disparaging remark about me or insult me, perhaps in jest, perhaps not. I not only retaliate, but escalate the insult; I insult you more strongly than you did me. You then up the ante even more by insulting me further or perhaps disparaging me to other people. You try to justify yourself to others by claiming I am the one that has caused all the trouble, and I do the same. This series of events continues to escalate until there are serious hard feelings, broken relationships, or worse. This sort of thing goes on from the time we are in kindergarten until the day we die. We have all experienced these situations and have lost friends, had strained relationships with family members or have had at least a temporarily troubled marriage as a result. The way to avoid these problems is to refuse to retaliate early on.

If I don't respond in kind to your disparaging remark or insult, the chain of events may well end there. There may be some truth to the insult or disparaging remark, and if I accept it in humility or respond with humor or even just say nothing in response, the dispute may be over before it begins. This, of course, is not easy. But look at the examples that Jesus gave. One of the things that was very difficult for the Jews of Jesus' day was that they lived in an occupied land. The Roman army controlled their land and a Roman soldier could impress any Jew into service at any time to do a task for the Romans. This is what is referred to when Jesus says "if anyone forces you to go one mile, go also the second mile." This is not something those present would have wanted to hear from Jesus, but there it is. Jesus was showing them as plainly as could be shown the extent to which they were to go to avoid retaliation. "Turning the other cheek" meant that they should not respond to an insult. Thus, the poisonous escalation of anger and retaliation is stopped.

Before going on to address how we can avoid retaliating, it is important to note what Jesus is *not* saying. He is not saying that you should allow someone to physically or emotionally harm you or abuse you. You are entitled to defend yourself if it comes to that. Furthermore, there is a difference between not retaliating and allowing someone to treat you without basic human decency. You are not expected to stay there and be someone's punching bag, either literally or figuratively. If you need to get the assistance of an authority figure, or even the law in some circumstances, you may do so. Despite our efforts and desire to live peaceably it is not always possible to do so with some people. As Paul said "If it is possible, *so far as it depends on you,* live peaceably with all." (Rom. 12:18)

So, how do we bring ourselves to the point of refusing to retaliate? For most of us, this is terribly difficult. Just telling ourselves we won't retaliate will not always work. Our emotions are just too strong and our tongues are too ready to respond in kind. The remedy Jesus offers is not one that is intuitively obvious, and would not have been to his listeners either. But if we truly want to be peacemakers (as we are commanded to do) and avoid retaliation, there is no other remedy. Jesus tells us— indeed, he commands us—to pray for those that are insulting us or speaking ill of us. This is difficult, but it is the only solution. Why? Because you cannot pray for someone and retain your anger against that person, at least not for long. Prayer is communion with God; when we go to God to ask the best for that person, our anger will dissipate and the urge to retaliate will also. It may take more than one prayer to release the anger and desire for revenge, but that is why we are urged to pray "at all times." (Eph. 6:18)

We may wish that Jesus had an easier solution for our finding peace. But praying for our enemies is part of being "sons of God." As Jesus points out, we are to do this "so that you may be children of your Father in heaven; for he makes his sun rise on the evil and on the good, and sends rain on the righteous and on the unrighteous." (Matt. 5:45) Through his common grace God blesses both the good and the bad with sunshine and rain, without which we could not have life. If God can do that for those who say worse things about him than are likely to be said about us, we can and should pray for our enemies. When we do that it will be easier to refrain from retaliating, and we will become peacemakers in our relationships with others.

There is, in addition, another role for us as peacemakers. We are not just to be peacemakers between ourselves and others; we are also to be peacemakers whenever possible between two or more other people. Whenever we can be a mediator between two other people in a dispute we should do so; it, too, is the work of "sons of God."

There are those in life who bring peace, and there are those in life who tend to stir up strife wherever they go. One of the worst examples of one who stirred things up is found in the aftermath of David's fall from grace. David had a beautiful daughter named Tamar, who was the sister of David's oldest son, Absalom. David also had another son named Amnon by another one of David's wives. Amnon apparently fell deeply in lust with Tamar, and was consumed over having her. Amnon took no action to fulfill his lust for Tamar, but he confided in his friend Jonadab who is described as "a very crafty man." (II Sam. 13:3) Jonadab concocted a ruse to get Tamar into Amnon's house and once she was there, Amnon raped her. After remaining silent for two years over what Amnon had done to his sister Tamar, Absalom took his revenge on Amnon by having him murdered during a feast that Absalom threw. (See II Sam. 13:1-39) By following the advice of his very crafty friend (and by never developing the core values that would get him through an attack of lust) Amnon came to an early and tragic end.

In most of the tragedies of William Shakespeare there is a character who stirred things up, who saw the tragic flaw in the lead character and helped bring about his downfall or demise. Perhaps the best known example was Iago who was both crafty and malicious in his manipulation of Othello. (William Shakespeare, "Othello, The Moor of Venice") He helped bring about the end of Othello's marriage to Desdemona and the death of both Othello and Desdemona. One of the reasons the plays of Shakespeare have spoken so strongly to generation after generation is his deep understanding and description of human nature, and the fact that all audiences recognize the character who stirs things up, who insures there will be no peace.

Jesus expects better things of us to make peace a reality in the lives of those with whom we come into contact. Especially among our family members and close friends we should always be mindful that we are to be agents of peace, not discord. The sad truth is that in many families there have been rifts that have lasted for decades, and no one has stepped forward to mediate a reconciliation between those whose relationship has been ruptured. If we are to truly be "sons of God" we must do our best to help bring reconciliation. It is not always possible to do so, but it is our duty to try.

There is a final aspect of bringing peace that must be addressed, and it applies both to our trying to bring peace to our own relationships and our trying to mediate peace between others. It is that peace and appeasement are not the same. God seeks reconciliation with us but not on just any terms; we must recognize the poverty of our spirit and we must repent, placing our faith in Jesus Christ. Likewise, as we seek to make peace with those with whom we have a dispute or an estranged relationship, we cannot do it on just any terms. We cannot violate our core values to bring peace. And we should not try to bring peace by simply saying that what they did to us doesn't matter, or that what we did to that person doesn't matter. If we have offended someone, it does matter, and we must make it right by apologizing and, if necessary, compensating them in some way. If they have offended us, we must be ready to forgive but not simply say it does not matter. That will only encourage more of the same. And we must not insist that the persons whose dispute we are attempting to mediate must violate their core values in the name of peace, even if we don't agree with their core values. This is part of treating every person with dignity and respect. Reconciliation will only be genuine and lasting if each person's dignity is respected. Otherwise, what has occurred is only appeasement and no lasting peace will result.

Most of us will never be preachers or teachers or full time Christian workers, but we can all be instruments of peace. If we do so, Jesus says we will be "sons of God."

The core value is:

*"I will do all I can to be at peace with others and to be an agent of peace among other people".*

## *QUESTIONS TO CONSIDER*

1.  Is peacemaking something that comes easy to you, or do you find it to be difficult? What is it that makes it easy or difficult?

2.  One of Jesus' instructions for making peace is to avoid retaliation when you have been insulted or wronged in some way. What are some of the ways you can go about avoiding retaliation? What is it that makes avoiding retaliation so difficult?

3.  Another of Jesus' instructions for being a peacemaker is that we pray for those who are insulting us or speaking evil of us. Have you sincerely tried this? How well has it worked? How can you become better at this?

4.  With regard to assisting other people in making peace when they have disputes or arguments, what do you believe are the best ways of doing this? Is it helpful that you remain neutral and not take sides in their dispute? Have you ever tried to impose your solution on others to resolve their dispute? How well has that worked?

5.  In the story mentioned in this chapter about Amnon raping his half sister, Tamar, Jonadab was the person who helped bring about the events that had tragic results for both Amnon and Tamar. If Jonadab had been a true friend, and one who desired to be a peacemaker, do you believe that this situation could have turned out differently? What do you think Jonadab should have done?

6.  Do you know anyone like Jonadab or like Iago (from "Othello, The Moor of Venice), who always stir things up, who insures that there will be no peace? How do you believe you should deal with someone like that? Have you ever seen any tendencies in yourself to stir things up and bring discord rather than peace? How do you think you should deal with those tendencies?

7.  Do you agree that peace and appeasement are not the same? Do you agree that we cannot violate our core values to bring peace and that we should not expect anyone else to violate his or her core

values to bring peace?  As a practical matter, how do you think this can be done?

# CHAPTER 10

# THE PERSECUTED
# ARE BLESSED

*"Blessed are those who are persecuted for righteousness' sake, for theirs is the kingdom of heaven." (Matt. 5:10)*

This appears to be perhaps the strangest of the beatitudes. Blessed are the persecuted? It is strange because although Jesus warned his disciples that they would be persecuted, just as he was persecuted (John 15:20), he did not extol persecution as something anyone should wish for. Nevertheless, Jesus, who was always candid with his disciples, warned them that there is a cost to discipleship (Luke 14:27-30) and they should expect difficulties and persecution.

But note that Jesus is not saying that all those who are persecuted will be blessed. There are many people in the world that have been persecuted for years, if not centuries. One can find minority groups on almost every continent that have suffered from the hands of a more powerful group, and continue to do so. However, it is not those groups to whom this beatitude is addressed.

Jesus is saying that it is only those "who are persecuted *for righteousness' sake*" that will be blessed. This was such an important issue to Jesus that he addressed it with his disciples on the night before he was crucified. He told them:

"If the world hates you, be aware that it hated me before it hated you. If you belonged to the world, the world would love you as its own. Because you do not belong to the world, but I have chosen you out of the world—therefore the world hates you. Remember the word that I said to you, 'Servants are not greater than their master.' If they persecuted me, they will persecute you." (John 15:18-20)

When we consider these words of Jesus carefully they remind us that being a Christian is serious business. In Chapter 6, we addressed Jesus' commandment that we give him first priority, that we should "hunger and thirst for righteousness." In this beatitude he tells us that if we pursue the righteousness that we hunger and thirst for, the result may be persecution. Furthermore, the persecution will come precisely because we are becoming righteous; in other words we are in a right relationship with God. His priorities and purposes are becoming our priorities and purposes, and we are beginning to live the core values that Jesus taught. So, he is clearly forewarning us, as he forewarned the disciples the night before his crucifixion, that not everyone will be pleased with our giving God first priority and attempting to abide in Jesus.

Why is this so? Why should the "world" be so upset with us and even be willing to persecute us in some way when we take our faith seriously and live according to Jesus' values? It is because the world does not share Jesus' values. The primary core value of the world is "I want what I want when I want it." The world does not want to hear about the poverty of our spirits or the need to repent. It certainly is not enamored with the idea of a God who demands that he be our first priority, regardless of the cost, one who expects us to abide in him. After all, if the world does not recognize that it has a "poverty of spirit" problem, it is not going to be interested in listening to what Christians have to say about how to deal with that poverty of spirit, or the consequences if they do not. This should come as no surprise to us; Jesus warned us that just as they did not welcome him or his message they will not always welcome us either, or the values that we attempt to live by.

Having said this, however, we must admit that persecution of Christians is not a major problem in our society. There are, in my opinion, two primary reasons for this. The first reason is that more people accept Christian values, at least on the surface, in our country than in many other countries because of the legacy of many of the early settlers, such as the Pilgrims, coming to America to escape religious persecution, and the legacy of the faithfulness of most of the founders of our country. I am certainly not contending that they were perfect; they were not. But they upheld traditional Christian values as the norm for society, without imposing those values on anyone. They also encouraged religious tolerance and believed that all should be free to worship or not worship as each person chose. It is true that they had some serious blind spots—such as slavery—but there is to this day a general acceptance, or at least tolerance, for someone taking his faith seriously. There is less such tolerance and acceptance in most other countries, even including those of western Europe, where a large portion of the population no longer gives a high priority to church attendance, much less to hungering and thirsting after righteousness in the manner Jesus expects.

The second reason that persecution of Christians in our society is not a problem is not as benign as the first reason. The truth is that most Christians in the United States do not live much differently than those who do not claim to be Christian. The values that we Christians live by are often the values of the broader culture and not those that Jesus taught. As Jesus said, "If you belonged to the world, the world would love you as its own." If our values are no different from the values of the world, why should they persecute us? They will love us. As long as we simply say everyone should just love one another (without getting into much detail about what that really means) and accept the world's argument that religion is a private matter that should not affect the public square, there is nothing for the world to dislike.

As mentioned in Chapter 1, the problem that Charles and Rachel had is that they, due to ignorance, indifference or self-centeredness, adopted the values of the world rather than the values of Jesus. They had never developed an internal set of values that would guide them through the temptations and hard choices in life. Charles recognized that what he was doing was wrong, but never came to the point of repentance. His desire to have everything he wanted in life overcame the commitment he made as a Christian to live in conformity with what Jesus taught. Rachel put her own desire for fulfillment ahead of her commitment to Christ (and her commitment to her parents) in making the decision to move in with Roger, and later with Steve. The priorities and values of Charles and Rachel are unfortunately far too common among Christians in our society today and will seldom lead to persecution by the world. What Charles received was not persecution but basic justice for his illegal acts.

Persecution should not be sought, but if it comes, it will only come when we live differently from the world and challenge the basic values of the world. That will only happen when we begin to change, to become more Christ-like in our values and in our behavior. When that occurs we may find that some of those who were our friends are no longer our friends, or some of those who were willing to do business with us or socialize with us are no longer willing to do so. Make no mistake, when that occurs there will be pain associated with it. That is part of the cost of discipleship. It will seem that there is truth to the old adage that "no good deed goes unpunished." Jesus is telling us to get ready for such treatment because it may well come.

However, Jesus is also telling us something else. When this occurs we should recognize it for what it is. We are really changing; our character is being molded into the character of Christ (although never perfectly). And that is something to rejoice over. We live in a culture of shallow values that encourages instant gratification and self-centered living. When we begin to live as Jesus taught, we leave the shallow values and self-centered living of this world behind; our frame of reference becomes not just the here and now, but the rest of this life and the life to come. When such profound change occurs in our lives it is worth the suffering we may have to endure. So, we rejoice not over the suffering itself but over the fact we are becoming more like Jesus, and the suffering is the proof of that. We are deemed worthy of suffering for the cause of Christ.

Yes, I know. This sounds strange; it may even seem to be convoluted reasoning to you. But read about the reaction of the Apostles to the suffering they endured when they began to preach that Jesus was the messiah, the Son of God. (Acts 5:17-42) The high priest strictly ordered them not to teach in the name of Jesus, but they did so anyway, and were punished for it by flogging. Luke, the author of the book of Acts, notes that "As they (the Apostles) left the council, they rejoiced that they were considered worthy to suffer dishonor for the sake of the name (of Christ)." (Acts 5:41) The Apostles had given Jesus first priority in their lives, and the persecution they received as a result was not something to bemoan (although it was painful) but rather something to rejoice over because they took this as proof that they were being obedient.

Undoubtedly, they remembered the words of Jesus:

"Blessed are you when people revile you and persecute you and utter all kinds of evil against you falsely on my account. Rejoice and be glad, for your reward is great in heaven, for in the same way they persecuted the prophets who were before you." (Matt. 5:11-12)

Finally, note the promise that comes with this beatitude: "for theirs is the kingdom of heaven." (Matt. 5:10) It is the same promise that comes with the first beatitude when we recognize the poverty of our spirit. Why is that? Because when we recognize the poverty of our own spirit we glimpse a new way of life in the kingdom of heaven. When we change from the way we were to the way we must become to live in harmony and fellowship with God, we begin to live in the kingdom of heaven. The persecution that follows is simply part of what those who have followed God over the centuries have suffered. As Jesus points out, this does not go unnoticed to him. He tells us to "Rejoice and be glad, *for your reward is great in heaven . . . .*" The suffering is worth it, for the rewards of living in the kingdom of heaven are great.

Thus, the core value is:

*"I will not be afraid to live righteously, despite persecution, and will rejoice if I am persecuted for following Jesus."*

## *QUESTIONS TO CONSIDER*

1. Have there been instances in your life in which you felt that you were being persecuted because of your beliefs or because you are a Christian? How did that make you feel? How did you respond to it? After reading this chapter, do you have any different view of what happened? Please explain.

2. This chapter causes us to focus on the cost of discipleship. Have you ever thought before about the cost of discipleship? Do you believe that you have experienced this cost of discipleship before? In what way?

3. In this chapter is the statement that "the world does not share Jesus' values." What are some of the differences in the values of the world and the values that Jesus taught? Do you know anyone who has been persecuted in some way over those differences in values?

4. Christians in the United States today are not persecuted in the same way that they were by the Roman government in the early days of the church. What are some of the ways in which Christians may experience some form of persecution in America today? Have you ever experienced this type of persecution?

5. Do you agree or disagree with the statement in this chapter that "most Christians in the United States do not live much differently than those who do not claim to be Christian?" If you disagree, what

are the two or three main ways in which you believe Christians live differently? If you agree with the statement, do you believe it is because most people in the United States have adopted Christian values, or do you believe that Christians are not living what they proclaim to believe? Please explain your answer.

6. How do you really feel about the idea of rejoicing when you are persecuted for being a Christian? Do you think that you will be able to do that, or will you become angry and bitter and take the attitude that "no good deed goes unpunished?" What can you do to have a proper perspective about the possibility of being persecuted for being a Christian?

# CHAPTER 11

# ANGER

*"But I say to you that if you are angry with a brother or sister, you will be liable to judgment; and if you insult a brother or sister, you will be liable to the council; and if you say, 'you fool,' you will be liable to the hell of fire." (Matt. 5:22)*

Having addressed the values inherent in the beatitudes, Jesus moved on to address certain other values that directly affect our behavior. We will address in future chapters some of the big issues—and sins to avoid—in the realm of Christian living. These include adultery, divorce, false swearing, almsgiving, prayer, faith and being judgmental, among others. Before addressing any of those topics, however, Jesus first addressed the topic of anger. There is, in my opinion, significance to the order in which Jesus presented the Sermon on the Mount. Before he gets into what we often think of as the "big sins" like adultery or dishonesty he addressed anger, which we often do not think of as a sin at all. Jesus, however, certainly did. He even likened it to murder. Let's look at what he said about anger:

"You have heard that it was said to those of ancient times, 'You shall not murder'; and 'whoever murders shall be liable to judgment.' But I say to you that if you are angry with a brother or sister, you will be liable to judgment; and if you insult a brother or sister, you will be liable to the council; and if you say, 'You fool,' you will be liable to the hell of fire. So when you are offering your gift at the altar, if you remember that your brother or sister has something against you, leave your gift there before the altar and go; first be reconciled to your brother or sister, and then come and offer your gift. Come to terms quickly with your accuser while you are on the way to court with him, or your accuser may hand you over to the judge, and the judge to the guard, and you will be thrown into prison. Truly I tell you, you will never get out until you have paid the last penny." (Matt. 5:21-26)

One of the reasons we have difficulty with the idea of anger being sinful is that the gospels clearly say that Jesus was, upon occasion, angry. When a man with a withered hand was brought to Jesus on a sabbath, Jesus was angry at the hardness of the hearts of the Pharisees who preferred to see the man not be healed rather than have Jesus heal him on the sabbath. (Mark 3:1-6) When Jesus drove the money changers from the temple, the scriptures do not explicitly state that Jesus was angry, but his words and actions indicate that he was. (Matt. 21:12-13) Similarly, Jesus denounced the scribes and Pharisees with language so strong (see Matt. 23:1-36) that he was obviously angry with them:

"But woe to you, scribes and Pharisees, hypocrites! For you lock people out of the kingdom of heaven. For you do not go in yourselves, and when others are going in, you stop them. Woe to you, scribes and Pharisees, hypocrites! For you cross sea and land to make a single convert, and you make the new convert twice as much a child of hell as yourselves." (Matt. 23:13-15)

How can we reconcile these actions of Jesus with his comparing anger to murder? It is because Jesus was referring not to the momentary or short term anger that afflicts us all from time to time, but the anger that we hold on to and refuse to release. Furthermore, in each of the instances mentioned above, Jesus was not angry over some wrong or slight to himself but rather at the hard, uncompassionate hearts of the Pharisees and scribes, their profaning the temple and their distortion of the scriptures. In other words, it was a *righteous* anger. When he had good grounds for anger over the unjust treatment that he personally received in both Jewish and Roman courts that resulted in his crucifixion, his response was quite different; it was simply "Father, forgive them; for they do not know what they are doing." (Luke 23:34)

Jesus spoke out so strongly against anger in the Sermon on the Mount because he understood that holding on to our anger is as damaging to our souls as cancer is to the body. Anger that we hold on to becomes frozen and leads to bitterness. It remains within us and slowly spreads from the initial target of our anger to most, if not all, aspects of our lives. Like cancer, anger metastasizes throughout our personality and our spirit and interferes with our relationships, our attitude toward life and our relationship with God.

In my own work I have seen the damage that anger has caused to family relationships. Part of my practice as a trial lawyer involves probate litigation. Probate litigation typically involves disputes over whether a deceased person had the testamentary capacity to execute a will (usually shortly before his or her death) or whether some person, oftentimes a family member, exercised "undue influence" over the deceased to cause him to leave most, if not all, of his assets to the person exercising the undue influence rather than it going equally to all the children, or as it had been agreed to previously. In many of these cases, there are rifts or grudges between brothers and sisters that go all the way back to middle school, although the brothers and sisters are now in their sixties. Their anger has sustained the rift over a period of 50 years or more and bitterness has set in to such a degree that any mending of the relationship is almost impossible. Jesus clearly says in the passage above that we will be liable to judgment for holding on to our anger against a brother or sister.

These words at first seem unduly harsh, especially coming from Jesus. But he is pointing out that murder has always been prohibited in the law (Exodus 20:13), and the consequence of our holding on to our anger against someone is, in God's eyes, almost as bad. Just before these verses Jesus instructed that we should be pure in heart. Holding on to our anger destroys the purity of our heart because in our heart we want not what is best for the object of our anger, but what is worst for him. Jesus commands us to pray for our enemies (Matt. 5:43-44) and retaining our anger against our enemies is a method of hating them. Thus, Jesus likens retained or frozen anger to murder. Both wish ill for the other person. We cannot abide in Jesus while simultaneously holding fast to our anger against anyone. Just as a murderer is liable to judgment, so also is she who holds on to her anger against another.

Another result of our anger toward another person is that it may cause us to treat him with contempt. We may insult someone out of anger or, worse, treat her contemptuously. Jesus does not mince words over our being so contemptuous of someone that we say "you fool" or equivalent words. When we allow our anger to carry us so far from the heart of God that we insult and treat others with contempt, Jesus says that we will be in danger of the fire of hell. (Matt. 5:22) To Jesus, this is serious indeed, and therefore it should be to us as well.

As mentioned above, Jesus is not speaking here of the momentary flashes of anger that we all have from time to time, or even the anger that lingers for a moment. As Paul said to the Ephesians "Be angry but do not sin; do not let the sun go down on your anger." (Eph. 4:26) In other words, the anger must be released, and we must release it promptly.

Jesus emphasized how important this is by saying "So when you are offering your gift at the altar, if you remember that your brother or sister has something against you, leave your gift there before the altar and go; first be reconciled to your brother or sister, and then come and offer your gift." (Matt. 5:23-24) The act of presenting gifts at the altar was central to Jewish worship, and worship at the temple was the highest priority for Jews. But Jesus commands that we first reconcile with our brother or sister and expunge the anger that has led to the breach before we offer the gift. Jesus well knew that true worship only comes from a pure heart (Ps. 24:4) and a heart that is full of anger or contempt for another cannot "worship the Father in spirit and truth." (John 4:23) Unless we release the anger and reconcile with those who were the objects of our anger we simply cannot expect to be in a right relationship with God.

Furthermore, the longer we hold on to our anger the more likely it is that our anger will lead to a host of other sins. Anger is a vice that continually harms us. Over time, anger leads to bitterness, to resentment, to a lack of love, to a lack of forgiveness and ultimately to indifference to God. No wonder Jesus compares it to murder. But notice who it is that is being killed. Ultimately it is we ourselves who suffer the consequences of our anger, more so than the person against whom our anger was originally directed. It leads to spiritual and emotional death. Just as cancer that is untreated kills the body from the inside, the anger that we hold on to and nurture will kill our spirit and our emotional well-being.

We simply must learn to deal with anger or we will never be able to deal with the other sins that we will discuss in future chapters. Jesus gives the analogy of one who is on the way to court and urges us to come to terms with our accuser before we get to court or the consequences may be dire (Matt. 5:25-26). From my own experience as a trial lawyer I can tell you that many of the cases that are tried in our courts are driven by anger more than the pursuit of justice. A verdict from a jury may result in a monetary recovery but it will not take away the anger in one's heart. And that anger will continue to eat away at the person's heart, regardless of the outcome of the case, until he releases that anger.

We cannot leave the topic of anger without addressing precisely how we go about releasing the anger. As we discussed in chapter 9 regarding being a peacemaker, we must learn to pray for those with whom we are angry, and we must pray that God will take away our anger. Do not expect this to be easy. If we are angry with someone, the last thing that we feel like doing is praying for the person with whom we are angry. We want to savor the delicious feeling of giving in to our anger and letting it have its way with us. We imagine all sorts of bad things happening to or being said to that person. But we should recognize that this is just further evidence of the poverty of our spirit, of our unwillingness to repent and to try to have a pure heart. When anger comes, warning sirens should go off in our heads telling us that now is the time that we most need to pray. We will address prayer further in chapter 18, but it is sufficient for our purposes now to recognize that we will be unable to overcome the power that anger can have over us unless we learn to promptly go to God in prayer when anger wells up within us.

Again, our example is Jesus. He had more than sufficient reasons to be angry at the scribes and Pharisees, at his own disciples who abandoned him when he was arrested (Mark 14:43-50), and even his own family who early in his ministry thought he had lost his mind (Mark 3:20-21). But Jesus refused to get angry, or in any event to retain any anger except possibly for the righteous anger he felt, as mentioned above. We, too, must promptly release our anger and "not let the sun go down on our anger." (Eph. 4:26)

The core value is:

*"I will promptly release my anger before God and will not hold on to it no matter what anyone does to me."*

## *QUESTIONS TO CONSIDER*

1. What kind of experiences with anger have you had? Were you able to release your anger, or are you still harboring it? If you were not able to release your anger, what effect did it have on you?

2. Before reading this chapter did you consider holding on to your anger to be a sin? How do you view anger now? How do you intend to deal with your anger now?

3. Do you personally know people who are filled with anger? What effect has that anger had on that person? On his/her personality? On his/her ability to maintain relationships?

4. Are there people whom you have treated with contempt? Did those feelings of contempt arise out of your anger? Do you still have those feelings toward anyone else? If not, how did you deal with your anger and contempt? If you still have those feelings toward someone, how are you going to deal with it?

5. Have you ever prayed for someone with whom you are angry? What effect did the act of praying for that person have on your anger? If you have never prayed for someone with whom you were angry before, are you willing to begin doing so now?

6. Have you begun to examine your own behavior during your devotional time each day to see what your behavior says about your true core values? If not, please consider doing so. What has your behavior told you about whether you have an anger problem and whether you are dealing with it appropriately?

# CHAPTER 12

# MARRIAGE/SEXUAL PURITY

*"You have heard that it was said, 'You shall not commit adultery.' But I say to you that everyone who looks at a woman with lust has already committed adultery with her in his heart." (Matt. 5:27-28)*

If there is any teaching of Jesus that runs counter to the tide of modern western culture, it is his teaching regarding marriage and sexual purity. The unavoidable truth is that we live in a sex-obsessed culture that uses sexual themes or images to sell products or services, to claim "sophistication," to create social status, or simply to entertain. Anyone who raises a cautionary word against such uses of sex is usually promptly labeled a prude and perhaps held up to ridicule. This tactic appears to be working, because anyone speaking out against the widespread use of sexual themes or images usually begins his defense by saying "I'm not a prude, but..."

Again, the order in which Jesus presented the topics addressed in the Sermon on the Mount comes into play. Before he addressed the issues of sex, marriage and divorce, he addressed hungering and thirsting for righteousness, and being pure in heart. He also addressed anger first, which may be a significant factor in a man or woman's decision to seek a divorce. We need to keep Jesus' teaching on these topics in mind as we examine what Jesus taught regarding sex, marriage and divorce.

Jesus' words in Matthew 5:27 that "You have heard that it was said, 'You shall not commit adultery,'" refers to the seventh of the Ten Commandments, which Jesus quoted verbatim: "You shall not commit adultery." (Exodus 20:14)   The definition of adultery is sexual inter-course between a man and a woman, at least one of whom is married to someone else.   There was a tendency within the Jewish leaders of Jesus' day to limit this prohibition strictly to improper sexual activity by one who was married.  They also did not believe that one's thought life could violate this commandment, which is strange given the language of the tenth commandment ("You shall not covet your neighbor's wife . . .") (Exodus 20:17)   In short, they tended to limit the degree of constraint that the Ten Commandments placed on one's behavior. (Though not all were in accord.  A strong minority led by Rabbi Shammai was particu-larly strict on grounds for divorce, limiting the grounds for divorce to unchastity.   Given human nature, Rabbi Shammai's view always remained a minority view).

Jesus cut through the technical definitions of adultery and said that God is interested not only in the observance of the letter of the law, but also the spirit of the law.  Having just set forth the expected standard of a pure heart by one hungering and thirsting for righteousness, Jesus declared that adultery begins with lust in the eye, not with the physical act of adultery.  Moreover, he doesn't limit the lustful look to those who are married, but to "everyone who looks at a woman with lust. . . ." Thus, Jesus' prohibition includes the unmarried as well as the married. One who wishes to abide in Jesus cannot live an undisciplined, sala-cious thought life while expecting Jesus to leave that part of the person's life unexamined.

To modern ears, this teaching of Jesus seems too restrictive.  Does Jesus really mean we can't even look?  (And this applies to girls and women looking at boys and men just as much as the other way around). No, the prohibition is not against looking, but looking "with lust."  There is a big difference between looking at someone of the opposite sex with a due appreciation of that person's attractiveness and lusting after that person. I don't have to explain the difference; you know the difference.

Amnon, the son of David, lusted after Tamar, his half sister (II Sam. 13:1-19). His lust, which was so strong it made him ill, led to his raping her. Once she saw what Amnon had in mind, Tamar pleaded with Amnon to ask David to let Amnon have her as a wife, but he was not interested in having her as a wife; she had become just a sexual object to him. Once he had satisfied his lust, scripture tells us that "Then Amnon was seized with a very great loathing for her; indeed, his loathing was even greater than the lust he had felt for her." (II Sam. 13:15) He kicked her out, leaving her in shame, and generating in Tamar's brother, Absalom, the plot to murder Amnon.

Jesus addresses how we avoid the casual look turning into a lustful look. And his advice shows just how seriously he views avoiding lust:

> "If your right eye causes you to sin, tear it out and throw it away; it is better for you to lose one of your members than for your whole body to be thrown into hell. And if your right hand causes you to sin, cut it off and throw it away; it is better for you to lose one of your members than for your whole body to go into hell." (Matt. 5:29-30)

Strong words, indeed. Why are there not more one-eyed and one-handed Christians? Fortunately for us, Jesus was using hyperbole to make a very important point, much as he did when he said, in explaining the cost of discipleship, "Whoever comes to me and does not hate father and mother, wife and children, brothers and sister, yes, and even life itself, cannot be my disciple." (Luke 14:26) Jesus did not literally mean that we must hate family, but he is telling us to get our priorities in order. In the passage about lust, he is saying we must take seriously his admonition to avoid lust. If it means not looking to avoid looking with lust, that is what we must do. Although I doubt there are many today who would take this passage literally, it is comforting to know that the Council of Nicea in 325 A.D. prohibited the practice of self-mutilation to comply with this scripture. Jesus does not want mutilation; he wants serious disciples who will give first priority to being obedient to him and who will seek to be pure in heart.

Paul followed up on Jesus expanding the prohibition against sexual sin to apply to the unmarried. In his first letter to the church at Corinth, a city notorious for debauchery, Paul instructed:

> "Shun fornication! Every sin that a person commits is outside the body, but the fornicator sins against the body itself. Or do you not know that your body is a temple of the Holy Spirit within you, which you have from God, and that you are not your own? For you were bought with a price; therefore, glorify God in your body." (I Cor. 6:18-20)

Inherent in the teaching of Jesus, and of Paul, is the standard that sexual intercourse is appropriate only within the marriage relationship. Otherwise, it is sin. Persistent sexual sin, as any other persistent sin, interferes with our spiritual growth and weakens our character. Just as we must take seriously Jesus' words that we addressed in previous chapters, we must likewise take seriously Jesus' words regarding sexual sin. The consequences if we do not are both spiritual and temporal. Rachel ignored Jesus' words regarding sexual sin, and it led her into two separate relationships with men that ended with her being an unwed mother struggling to care for two young girls who will grow up without a father.

The consequences of ignoring Jesus' teaching on sexual sin is also becoming increasingly apparent in society at large. A recent report found that approximately 26 percent of young women ages 14 to 19 in the United States have at least one of the most common sexually transmitted diseases. (The Orlando Sentinel, January 4, 2009, citing the Centers for Disease Control and Prevention) And according to the National Center for Health Statistics, about 40 percent of all births in the United States in 2007 were to unwed mothers. These statistics are heartbreaking, and they demonstrate once more that when we abandon

God's values in our lives, the consequences can be painful to us as individuals and also to us collectively as a nation.

Just as Jesus raised the bar on sexual purity, he also raised the standard for marriage. According to William Barclay, the Scottish Biblical scholar and historian, the state of marriage among the Romans and the Greeks at the time of Jesus' ministry was deplorable. Extramarital relationships by Greek and Roman men were not only accepted but expected. Divorce was as common as marriage, and it was not uncommon for a man or a woman to be married and divorced multiple times. (See William Barclay, *The Gospel of Matthew, Vol. One, pp 176-181*, Westminster John Knox Press).

Theoretically at least, the state of marriage was much stronger among the Jews of Jesus' day, but the poisonous effects of the Greek and Roman view of marriage had crept into Jewish life, and divorce was becoming increasingly common. There was a debate among the rabbis as to how strict the grounds for divorce must be. Rabbi Hillel led the liberal view which permitted divorce for almost any reason whatsoever; Rabbi Shammai led the conservative view which permitted divorce only for unchastity. (See, id., pp. 173-176).

It is against this background that Jesus' teaching on marriage and divorce was given. Jesus clearly came down on the high view of marriage. He said:

> "It was also said, 'Whoever divorces his wife, let him give her a certificate of divorce.' But I say to you that anyone who divorces his wife, except on the grounds of unchastity, causes her to commit adultery; and whoever marries a divorced woman commits adultery." (Matt. 5:31-33)

Jesus also addressed this topic in Matthew 19:

> "Some Pharisees came to him, and to test him they asked, 'Is it lawful for a man to divorce his wife for any cause?' He answered, 'Have you not read that the one who made them at the beginning 'made them male and female' and said, 'For this reason a

man shall leave his father and mother and be joined to his wife, and the two shall become one flesh'? So they are no longer two, but one flesh. Therefore what God has joined together, let no one separate.' They said to him, 'Why then did Moses command us to give a certificate of dismissal and to divorce her?' He said to them, 'It was because you were so hard-hearted that Moses allowed you to divorce your wives, but from the beginning it was not so. And I say to you, whoever divorces his wife, except for unchastity, and marries another commits adultery.'" (Matt. 19:3-9)

Thus, Jesus clearly upheld the strict view that marriage should be held in high esteem and a marriage should not be ended by divorce except for unchastity, namely adultery. This standard may seem unduly strict to modern ears but it did also to Jesus' own disciples. As Matthew 19 points out:

"His disciples said to him, 'If such is the case of a man with his wife, it is better not to marry.' But he said to them, 'Not every-one can accept this teaching, but only those to whom it has been given.'" (Matt. 19:10-11)

The issue of what constitutes acceptable grounds for divorce has been a contentious one within the church for many years. Even those who may be more liberal in permitting divorce usually still acknowl-edge that it is a serious and tragic event, contrary to God's plan. The high divorce rate today is further evidence of the poverty of our spirit and our need for repentance. There is seldom a truly innocent party in any divorce.

Jesus' teaching concerning marriage and divorce should cause anyone contemplating marriage to consider solemnly the decision he or she is about to make. Romance alone is not a sufficient reason for a man and woman to marry. Rachel was sure she had found "true love" with Steve and her relationship with him turned out no better than her relationship with Roger. Marriage should be entered into only after an appropriate amount of time, and considerable thought and prayer. A good marriage is one of God's greatest blessings, but an inadvisable marriage that leads to divorce leaves many wounds, not only among the marriage partners but among their children as well. With God's grace one can recover from those wounds, but it is better to avoid them if one can.

The core value is:

*"I will live a sexually pure life and avoid sexual sin. If married, I will honor and cherish my spouse and do all I can to avoid divorce."*

## QUESTIONS TO CONSIDER

1. One of the key issues that young people will have to face in life, and often before their mid-teens, is whether they will engage in sexual activity. What signals do you believe our society (the world) sends to young people about sexual activity?

2. Do you believe that it is possible for older teens and adults in their 20s and 30s to have meaningful relationships with the opposite sex without engaging in sexual activity? What do you believe are the key factors in maintaining meaningful relationships with the opposite sex without engaging in sexual activities? What core values should you be looking for in a close friend of the opposite sex to help you avoid becoming involved in a sexual relationship?

3. What do you think about Jesus' admonition not to look at a woman (or a man) "with lust?" Is this a problem for you? How do you think you should go about avoiding looking at someone "with lust"?

4. In the story about Amnon and Tamar (II Sam. 13:1-19) mentioned in this chapter, the scriptures tell us that after he raped Tamar Amnon "was seized with a very great loathing for her; indeed, his loathing was even greater than the lust he had felt for her." What

does this tell you about the nature of lust? What does it tell you about how to deal with lust?

5.  In this chapter is a quote from Paul from I Cor. 6:18-20 in which Paul says "the fornicator sins against the body itself." What do you think Paul means by that? If you have been involved in sexual activity outside the marriage relationship, how did that sexual activity make you feel about yourself? Have you prayed about your sexual sins and asked God to forgive you and strengthen you in this area?

6.  What do you think about the statement in this chapter that "Romance alone is not a sufficient reason for a man and woman to marry"? What other factors do you believe are necessary for a good marriage? Are there any specific core values that you are looking for in a spouse? Why are you looking for those specific core values? If you are already married, what core values of yours and your spouse have been most helpful to your marriage?

7.  What are the primary things that you believe that you and your spouse should do to insure that your marriage will not end in divorce?

# CHAPTER 13

# HONESTY

*"Again, you have heard that it was said to those of ancient times, 'You shall not swear falsely, but carry out the vows you have made to the Lord.' But I say to you, Do not swear at all . . . . Let your word be 'Yes, Yes' or 'No, No'; anything more than this comes from the evil one."* (Matt. 5:33-34, 37)

The intent of this passage is not immediately apparent. It appears to be about vows, which are seldom used today in the same way they were used in biblical times. In addressing the problems with the rules regarding vows, as those rules then existed, Jesus was really addressing the underlying issue of whether one's word could be relied upon.

The issue of misusing the name of the Lord is addressed in the Ten Commandments. The Third Commandment states: "You shall not make wrongful use of the name of the Lord your God, for the Lord will not acquit anyone who misuses his name." (Ex. 20:7) We usually think of this commandment as merely prohibiting profanity; however, it prohibits not only that but also using the Lord's name to add solemnity to a promise that one does not intend to keep. In effect, this commandment says "Do not make the Lord a party to your lies, broken promises and misrepresentations." If we make a vow using the name of the Lord, that vow is solemn and must be kept.

Likewise, the ninth commandment forbids any type of false or misleading statements against another person. "You shall not bear false witness against your neighbor." (Ex. 20:16)  Although this prohibition would include any type of judicial or similar proceeding, it is not limited to such a proceeding.  A Christian should not bear false witness under any circumstances toward any other person.

The foregoing prohibitions in the Ten Commandments seem fairly straight forward.  They demand that we avoid any type of dishonesty in dealing with others, and that we be scrupulously honest in any statements regarding another person.  This is part of the basic character that is expected of anyone claiming to be a follower of Christ.  The problem was that the Jews, and particularly the scribes and Pharisees, had developed a set of loopholes to these commandments that basically held that one had to adhere to this standard of honesty only if a certain type of vow was made; otherwise, any promises could be broken and any statements of the speaker could stray far from the truth.  Jesus rebuked the scribes and Pharisees for this practice, using some of the strongest language found in the gospels:

> "Woe to you, blind guides, who say, 'Whoever swears by the sanctuary is bound by nothing, but whoever swears by the gold of the sanctuary is bound by the oath.'  You blind fools!  For which is greater, the gold or the sanctuary that has made the gold sacred? And you say, 'Whoever swears by the altar is bound by nothing, but whoever swears by the gift that is on the altar is bound by the oath.'  How blind you are!  For which is greater, the gift or the altar that makes the gift sacred?  So whoever swears by the altar, swears by it and by everything on it and by the one who dwells in it; and whoever swears by heaven, swears by the throne of God and by the one who is seated upon it."  (Matt. 23:16-22)

In essence, the scribes and Pharisees had turned the reliability of one's word into a game of "Simon Says."  A person's word was only reliable if he uttered the magic words approved by the scribes and Pharisees; otherwise one was free to ignore what he had just promised to do, even if he had sworn an oath invoking the altar of the Lord to convince the person to whom he was speaking that he really meant it.

There is nothing more harmful to the development of godly character than the kinds of fraudulent gamesmanship that the scribes and Pharisees were tolerating if not encouraging. Jesus wanted none of it:

> "But I say to you, Do not swear at all, either by heaven, for it is the throne of God, or by the earth, for it is his footstool, or by Jerusalem, for it is the city of the great King. And do not swear by your head, for you cannot make one hair white or black. Let your word be 'Yes, Yes' or 'No, No'; anything more than this comes from the evil one." (Matt. 5:34-37)

Do you see what Jesus is saying? If we do not mean what we say, if our word is not reliable, we are far from God. Anything other than strict honesty comes not from God, but from the evil one. Jesus wants us to abide in him. When we abide in him we act in conformity with his commandments, his character and his will. There is nothing more central to the character of Jesus than the truth. And he expects truth to be central to the character of his disciples. As he told his followers: "If you continue in my word, you are truly my disciples; and you will know the truth, and the truth will make you free." (John 8:32) One who seeks to live in the truth will not require an oath to speak the truth. His word is his bond.

It is instructive to note how seriously the early church took Jesus' admonition that his followers speak the truth. The story of Ananias and Sapphira is a cautionary lesson to any Christian who would compromise his honesty. (See Acts 5:1-11) In the early days of the church the believers that had property or other wealth sometimes sold their property or other valuable items and gave the proceeds to the church which would distribute the proceeds to those in need. They were so generous that scripture tells us that "There was not a needy person among them. . . ." (Acts 4:34) Ananias and his wife, Sapphira, sold a piece of property they owned, and brought part of the proceeds to the church and laid it at the apostles' feet. This was a good thing; however, Ananias and Sapphira told the apostles that they were giving the *entire* proceeds to the church when, in fact, they had held back part of the proceeds for themselves. There was absolutely nothing wrong with their holding back part of the proceeds for themselves (As Peter told them, "After it was sold, were not the proceeds at your disposal?" (Acts 5:4)) However, Ananias and Sapphira apparently wanted the church to think they were more generous or more spiritual than they actually were. They told the apostles that they had given the church the full sales price, which was a lie.

Peter confronted Ananias with the fact that he had been untruthful, and told him "you did not lie to us but to God." (Acts 5:4) Whereupon, Ananias promptly fell down and died. Some three hours later his wife arrived at the church, unaware of what had happened to her husband. Peter asked her what the purchase price was, and she also lied to Peter about the price, concealing the fact that she and her husband had held back part of the price for themselves while pretending otherwise. Upon Sapphira repeating the same lie her husband had told, Peter said to her "How is it that you have agreed together to put the Spirit of the Lord to the test? Look, the feet of those who have buried your husband are at the door, and they will carry you out." (Acts 5:9) Whereupon, Sapphira also fell down and died. She was buried beside her husband that same day. In one of the understatements of scripture, Acts tells us that "great fear seized the whole church and all who heard of these things." (Acts 5:11) Imagine the reaction if something like that happened in a modern church!

You may think that the consequences to Ananias and Sapphira were too harsh because they lied in the midst of giving a generous gift, even if it was not as generous as they claimed. However, Jesus will not tolerate half truths or lies from his disciples. As the Psalmist proclaimed:

"Who may dwell on
　　your holy hill?
Those who walk blamelessly,
　　and do what is right,
and speak the truth from
　　their heart." (Ps. 15:1-2)

If we want to abide in him we must not compromise with the truth. Our word must be our bond and all who know us must be able to trust us to tell the truth. When I was a cadet at the United States Air Force Academy I lived under the Cadet Honor Code: "We will not lie, steal or cheat, nor tolerate among us anyone who does." Far from being oppressive, it was a liberating experience living among those dedicated to such a high standard of honesty and truth. We also knew the consequences: if we violated the honor code, we would be expelled, no exceptions. As Christians we have an honor code that is just as absolute. Thankfully, our Lord is more forgiving, but we must make honesty such a strong part of our core values that we will never need forgiveness for being dishonest.

The failure to follow Jesus' words regarding basic honesty was what led to Charles Browne's downfall, and ultimately to his jail sentence. Cheating in school and cheating on his expense reimbursement statements did not seem all that significant to Charles. But ultimately there are no "little lies" or "little thefts." Once Charles began to compromise his basic integrity, he started down the path that finally derailed his life, leaving heartache, betrayal and misery in its wake.

One final point about oaths. Jesus was not making a blanket prohibition against oaths or vows under appropriate circumstances. In fact, at his own trial Jesus stated under oath that he was the Messiah, the Son of God. (Matt. 26:63-64) Paul also invoked an oath occasionally before God to emphasize the point he was making (II Cor. 1:23; Gal. 1:20). Paul's teaching was consistent with that of Jesus that a believer's word must be truthful and reliable regardless of whether he has sworn an oath.

The most common way one is called upon today to take an oath is as a witness in legal proceedings or perhaps to complete certain government forms. These oaths invoke the laws of perjury for those who are willing to lie under oath. The fact that one is called upon to take a solemn oath in legal proceedings should not be a stumbling block for the Christian. We must comply with the civil law, although we must feel equally bound before God to tell the truth even if we have not taken an oath before an officer to tell the truth. When we first make a commitment to follow Christ, we are, in effect, taking an oath to tell the truth at all times.

The core value is:

*"I will always be truthful; my word is my bond."*

## QUESTIONS TO CONSIDER

1. Honesty is something that everyone agrees with in principle, but we often want exceptions for ourselves, at least at times. Are there ever any circumstances in your life that you believe warrant your being dishonest or untruthful?

2. How do you feel about "little white lies?" Have you ever told any little white lies? Have you ever misled anyone with your little lies? What can you do to remind yourself to be truthful at all times?

3. How important is complete honesty with those that you are closest to, such as close friends or family members? What has been the effect on you when you have learned that a friend or family member was not truthful or was otherwise dishonest with you? Did you trust that person as much thereafter? Have you ever been dishonest or untruthful with a friend or family member? What was the result?

4. What does the story of Ananias and Sapphira tell you about how important honesty and truthfulness are to God? What was the problem that led to their dishonesty?

5. Do you agree with the statement at the end of this chapter that "When we first make a commitment to follow Christ, we are, in effect, taking an oath to tell the truth at all times?" Do you agree that as a Christian your word is your bond? Have you ever considered what another person may think about your Christian commitment if you are not truthful with that person?

# CHAPTER 14

# RETALIATION

*"You have heard that it was said, 'An eye for an eye and a tooth for a tooth.' But I say to you, Do not resist an evildoer. But if anyone strikes you on the right cheek, turn the other also; and if anyone wants to sue you and take your coat, give your cloak as well; and if anyone forces you to go one mile, go also the second mile. Give to everyone who begs from you, and do not refuse anyone who wants to borrow from you." (Matt 5: 38-42)*

We addressed the issue of retaliation in chapter 9 in the context of being a peacemaker. In this chapter we address the issue of retaliation in the context of Jesus' teaching about Christian love. As we shall see in this chapter and the next, the love that we as Christians are to give to others, and not just other Christians, goes far beyond the demands of the law given to Moses. If there are any chapters in this book that challenge our basic human instincts, they are this one and the next, as we can readily see by the examples that Jesus presents in the verses above.

Jesus begins by quoting a summary of the law given by Moses: "An eye for an eye and a tooth for a tooth." This is known as the *lex talionis*, or as William Barclay describes it, "the law of tit for tat." (William Barclay, *The Gospel of Matthew, Vol. One, p. 188,* Westminster John Knox Press) The *lex talionis* can be found in other ancient law codes, and is expressly set forth by Moses in the law that Israel was to follow: "If any harm follows, then you shall give life for life, eye for eye, tooth for tooth, hand for hand, foot for foot, burn for burn, wound for wound, stripe for stripe." (Ex. 21: 23-24) It is important to note that this was punishment that was to be extracted in courts of law. It was not the prerogative of an individual to extract that kind of punishment on his own.

Jesus quotes the standard of the law which was to be administered in courts of law, but then proceeds to set forth quite a different standard for the individual disciple to follow. The law demands justice, but Jesus says "Do not resist an evildoer." Whereas our natural tendency is to respond in kind to any wrong suffered or insult given, and likewise to return good for good and favor for favor, Jesus clearly says that is not the standard he expects us to follow. We are not to resist an evildoer. He gives three real life examples to explain the extent to which we are to go to not resist an evildoer, and, in addition, an example of how we are to respond to one who is not an evildoer but in need.

The first example is the best known: "Turn the other cheek." This is a reference to a backhanded slap across the face, which was not given to physically injure someone but rather to insult him. The natural tendency is to respond with a slap, or an insult, of our own. But Jesus instructs otherwise. He says to turn the other cheek, which means to absorb the insult without responding in kind. It is the opposite of retaliating. Perhaps the best modern example of someone who lived a life of non-retaliation was Martin Luther King. In fact, he made non-violent resistance the core of his strategy to confront racism and discrimination and to demand simple justice. He was insulted, imprisoned, and even physically assaulted, but refused to respond in kind. When the dogs were unleashed on Dr. King and the other marchers on the bridge in Selma, Alabama in 1965, there was finally a recognition throughout America (or most of it) of the evil of racism that retaliation in kind would not have brought.

Note that Jesus says "Do not resist an *evildoer.*" In refusing to retaliate we do not deny the evil; we simply follow Jesus' teaching and example not to retaliate. By refusing to retaliate and "turning the other cheek" we may shame the evildoer into confronting his evil actions. As we discussed in chapter 5, one who is humble is not a doormat, but one who is strong. Likewise, one who turns the other cheek and refuses to retaliate is stronger by far than the one who responds in kind. Who was stronger, those who released the dogs on the marchers, or Dr. King and the other marchers who refused to retaliate? Had Dr. King responded in kind to the violence perpetrated on him, he would not have had the powerful moral authority that is still so widely acknowledged today. Even though justice would have given him the right to retaliate to some degree, Dr. King, as a minister of the gospel of Jesus Christ, was fully aware of Jesus' command to turn the other cheek. We must likewise make non-retaliation one of our core values if we are to be serious about our Christian faith.

The second example goes even further to show how we are to respond to an evildoer. Jesus says: "If anyone wants to sue you and take your coat, give your cloak as well." (Matt. 5: 40) As a trial lawyer, this is an especially difficult passage for me to understand, but it appears to be closely related to Jesus' teaching in Matt. 5:25-26:

> "Come to terms quickly with your accuser while you are on the way to court with him, or your accuser may hand you over to the judge, and the judge to the guard, and you will be thrown into prison. Truly I tell you, you will never get out until you have paid the last penny."

In saying "if anyone wants to sue you and take your coat, give your cloak as well." Jesus seems to be emphasizing the extent to which one should go to avoid disputes, recriminations and retaliation. The "coat" or tunic was the bag-like inner garment that we have seen in movies set in Biblical times. The outer garment, or cloak, was heavier and could be used as an outer garment by day and as a blanket by which to keep warm as one slept at night. It was a critical garment and most people had only one cloak. Therefore, to give up one's cloak to avoid a lawsuit was truly loving one's enemy.

The point that Jesus is making is that one must be willing to give up something of great value to avoid allowing a dispute between two godly people to deteriorate to the extent they are adversaries in court. If two people who claim to be Christian wind up in court they have both already lost regardless of the outcome of the law suit. Remember, in God's eyes, money and possessions are clearly secondary to our being in a right relationship with him and our neighbor (Matt. 6:33). We must be willing to make sacrifices to keep those same priorities in our lives.

The third example Jesus gave would likely have been startling to his listeners. He said "If anyone forces you to go one mile, go also the second mile." (Matt. 5:41) This is a saying that does not resonate with modern listeners, at least not those living in western countries. It is a reference to the fact that the Jews then lived in an occupied territory. The occupying Roman army was ruthless and was generally despised by the Jews. One reason the Roman soldiers were so despised is that any Roman soldier had the right to impress any Jew into service simply by laying the flat of his sword on the Jew's shoulder and commanding him to do whatever task the Roman ordered. The best known example of this is that Simon of Cyrene was compelled by the soldiers leading Jesus to the cross to carry the cross on which Jesus would be crucified. (Matt. 27:32) Human nature being what it is, you can imagine how one would resent being forced to "go one mile" in service to a Roman soldier, the enemy of the Jews, and, in their eyes, the enemy of God.

Even under these extraordinary circumstances Jesus says that we should not resent the compelled service, but be willing to go beyond that which we are compelled to do. Although we are not likely to face an identical situation, we still are compelled by custom, business or family relationships, or by a variety of other circumstances, to do something for someone else that we do not particularly want to do. When those situations arise we should be willing to do not only the least expected of us, but more.

Note that Jesus does not say that we must actually *like* what we must do, but we must do it anyway in obedience to God as we demonstrate love for others, even love for our enemies. As you may have noticed from the chapter on repentance and the chapter on persecution, being obedient in the Christian life is sometimes difficult. It was difficult for Jesus as well as he carried out the mission he had been given. In the Garden of Gethsemane on the night before his crucifixion Jesus sweated "great drops of blood" (Luke 22:44) in his anguish over what lay ahead. Yet, he was obedient even in the face of the cross because his desire to be obedient was stronger than his anxiety over what lay ahead. It is not too much for God to ask us to "go also the second mile" to show the love of God to those for whom Jesus also died.

The final example does not pertain to an evildoer but rather to two other classes of people whose presence we usually do not welcome. Jesus tells us to "Give to everyone who begs from you, and do not refuse anyone who wants to borrow from you." (Matt. 5:42) To say that beggars are not welcome in most areas is an understatement. Most cities go to great lengths to keep beggars off the streets of the downtown areas. Even those who feel empathy for a beggar at a distance often become uncomfortable when the beggar approaches and asks for a handout. How often have you averted the eyes of a beggar to avoid having to give to him? As uncomfortable as it may be for us, Jesus' approach to beggars is simple: give. Why would he do this? Won't this just bring more beggars? Jesus wants everyone to know and experience the love of God. Just as God gives freely of his love to all, he wants us to do likewise. Our gift to a beggar may be all he has for the day. Or it may be all that stands between the belief that life is hopeless and the belief that there is hope after all. In chapter 7, we examined Jesus' statement that we are blessed if we are compassionate. By freely giving to those who ask we will become more compassionate. We need to give as much as the beggar needs to ask.

The second class of people Jesus mentions is those who want to borrow from us. Borrowers are often even less welcome than beggars. What do most people dislike more than a family member or friend wanting to borrow money? Again, it is our own attitude that Jesus says must change. He says we should not refuse anyone who wants to borrow from us. (I did mention previously that there is a cost of discipleship.) I confess that this is an issue with which I struggled for many years. Friends would ask to "borrow" money and I would lend it, usually because I would feel guilty if I did not lend the money in light of these verses. The friend would then usually not repay the loan. I would become resentful over his refusal (or more likely his inability) to pay me back, and the net result was that I felt worse than if I had not lent the money in the first place. I eventually came to the decision that I would lend money to a friend only if in my mind it was a gift. Although the other person may prefer to consider it a loan, to me it was a gift and therefore I would not be resentful if it was not repaid. I hope that I am not stretching Jesus' words beyond their intent, but this decision has made me more generous and more ready to lend.

Each person must decide for himself or herself how far one can go to give or to lend and we should not give or lend out of guilt. But clearly Jesus wants us to be generous, just as God has been generous with us. To the extent we have an abundance we should willingly share a portion of that abundance with those in need whether that person is a friend, an enemy or a stranger.

The core value is:

*"I will not retaliate against someone who insults me or wrongs me. Instead, I will pray for that person, treat him with respect and godly love, and be generous to him if he is in need."*

## QUESTIONS TO CONSIDER

1.  Why is the idea of not retaliating to a wrong or insult against us so difficult? Is it because we feel that we are not standing up for ourselves if we allow someone to wrong us without our retaliating? Have there been instances in your life that you refused to retaliate? If so, what was the result? Have there been instances in which you did retaliate? If so, what was the result?

2.  What did your parents teach you about not retaliating? If you have children (or younger brothers or sisters) what have you taught them about retaliation? How do you teach someone to be strong but not retaliate?

3.  Do you agree with the statement in this chapter that "one must be willing to give up something of great value to avoid allowing a dispute between two godly people to deteriorate to the extent they are adversaries in court?" What do you believe that you can do to avoid such a situation?

4.  Although we are not likely to be compelled into the service of another as the Jews were at the demand of the Romans, we are all likely to be asked to do something for others, perhaps family, friends or acquaintances, that we do not particularly want to do. Have you had such experiences? If so, did you "go the second mile?" What was the result? If your efforts were not appreciated, were you able to remind yourself that you do this in service to God, so man's response is not the most important thing?

5.  How do you feel about beggars asking you for money? Do you usually try to avoid them? What do you believe you can do to change your attitude towards beggars? If you have given to beggars, what effect has that had on you?

6.  How do you feel about friends or relatives wanting to borrow money from you? What can you do to change your attitude towards borrowers? If you have made loans to others before and not been paid back

how did you deal with that?  How do you think you should have dealt with that situation?

# CHAPTER 15

# CHRISTIAN LOVE

*"You have heard that it was said, 'You shall love your neighbor and hate your enemy.' But I say to you, Love your enemies and pray for those who persecute you, so that you may be children of your Father in heaven; for he makes his sun rise on the evil and on the good, and sends rain on the righteous and on the unrighteous. For if you love those who love you, what reward do you have? Do not even the tax collectors do the same? And if you greet only your brothers and sisters, what more are you doing than others? Do not even the Gentiles do the same? Be perfect, therefore, as your heavenly Father is perfect." (Matt. 5:43-48)*

These verses go to the heart of how differently Jesus expects us to live. The standard that he lays down is quite different from the standard of the world. Nevertheless, the world knows and understands that this is the standard for the Christian and will not hesitate to criticize one who claims to be a Christian but fails to live up to this standard.

Jesus begins with "You have heard that it was said 'You shall love your neighbor and hate your enemy'." This refers to a teaching by the scribes and Pharisees that was based upon Leviticus 19:18: "You shall not take vengeance or bear a grudge against any of your people, but you shall love your neighbor as yourself." The scribes and Pharisees assumed and therefore taught that the neighbor that they were to love as themselves was a fellow Jew. A fellow Jew was not an enemy, even if there were disagreements with him. Thus, the obligation to love one's neighbor as himself was limited to one who was of the same race and religion. The law was silent, they reasoned, with regard to enemies, so one was free to hate one's enemies. Thus, the commandment to love one's neighbor as himself found in Leviticus 19:18 morphed into "You shall love your neighbor and hate your enemy."

Before we get too critical of this teaching by the scribes and Pharisees, we should acknowledge that this is the standard that most people, even most Christians, follow in interpersonal relationships. We tend to love those who love us and dislike those who dislike us. Thus, we are usually friendly and benevolent with our friends and family and cool and distant, if not antagonistic, with those we perceive to be our enemies, or at least strangely different from us. If you are conservative in your political views do you treat political liberals as the neighbor you must love as yourself? If you are liberal in your political views how do you demonstrate to a conservative that you love her as you love yourself? The same questions could be asked regarding someone of another race, religion, nationality or ethnicity. The fact is that our natural instinct is to love those who love us (or at least agree with us) and dislike those who don't love us (or don't agree with us). In the vernacular, we tend to give as good (and as bad) as we get.

Jesus clearly labeled that standard as unacceptable to him ("Do not even the tax collectors do the same?") (Matt. 5:46). Instead, we are to love our enemies and pray for those who persecute us. On its face, this commandment of Jesus is even more difficult to swallow than Jesus' commandment to "turn the other cheek" when we are insulted. How can Jesus expect us to actually love our enemies? We might be able to tolerate our enemies, but loving them is going too far. The key to understanding what Jesus means is found in the definition of "love."

The Greek language in which the New Testament is written has several different words for love. We tend to associate strong feelings of romantic love or family love when we use the English word love, but the Greek words for love had a variety of different meanings. *Storge* was the

Greek word for family love—the love of a child for a parent or a parent for the child. *Eros* was the Greek word for romantic love or sexual love. It is the word from which we get the English word *erotic*. *Philia* is the Greek word used for the warm affection between true friends. You may recognize the similarity to the word *Philadelphia,* the city of friendly people.

Significantly, none of these words are attributed to Jesus when he says we must love our neighbor as ourselves. Jesus certainly does not expect us to have the same *feelings* for our enemy as we do for our closest friends and family. However, Jesus does expect us to treat our enemies with the same goodwill that God has shown to us. The Greek word used for love in these verses is *agape,* which denotes benevolence or goodwill. Regardless of how we are treated by our enemy or those who persecute us, we are to wish him well and act in his best interest without bitterness or resentment. As Jesus points out, by doing this we are following the example of God, who causes the sun to rise and the rain to fall on the righteous and the unrighteous alike. In his benevolence and his common grace, God grants these blessings to those who love him and also to those who despise him. We are to do the same with respect to those who are our enemies or our persecutors.

Jesus clearly taught that our neighbor is not just those whom we know and like, but those who could be included among our enemies. In the parable of the Good Samaritan (Luke 10:29-37), Jesus directly addressed the question "Who is the neighbor that we are to love as ourselves?" In this parable Jesus compared the treatment of the man on his way to Jericho, who was robbed and left for dead, by a priest, a Levite and a Samaritan. Only the Samaritan, whom Jews disdained (See John 4:9), had pity and stopped to aid him. Jesus specifically asked the lawyer who questioned him regarding the definition of *neighbor* "Which of these three, do you think, was a neighbor to the man who fell into the hands of the robbers?" (Luke 10:36) Even the lawyer had to admit it was "the one who showed him mercy." To which Jesus replied: "Go and do likewise." In other words, it is not enough just to *know* who is our neighbor; we must *act* like a neighbor by loving him as ourselves.

The difference between this kind of love and the love that we have for our spouse or boyfriend or girlfriend is that agape love is primarily an act of the will rather than an act of the heart. Whereas we may fall in love with our sweetheart, even if we did not intend to do so, we do not fall into agape love. It comes only as an act of the will, and usually only with much prayer and discipline. It is natural to "fall in love," but agape love does not come naturally; indeed, it is a gift of God that comes only as we earnestly desire it and ask God to give us the ability to love with agape love. By doing so, Jesus says we will become "children of your Father in heaven." In other words, we become more like God, who blesses both the righteous and the unrighteous.

But what does this mean, to love our neighbor as ourselves by treating him with the same goodwill and benevolence with which God treats saint and sinner alike? Does it mean that we must do whatever another person asks of us? Does it mean another person can do whatever he wishes to us without our ever resisting or ever raising an objection? The answer lies in the way a parent treats his or her child. The relationship in which most people show benevolence and goodwill is in the relationship between parent and child. But parents do not let their children do whatever they wish. Indeed, a large part of parenting is teaching children that they *cannot* do whatever they wish. It would be showing a lack of goodwill and benevolence to our children if we allowed them to believe they could always behave just as they pleased. Similarly, we must sometimes show our goodwill by holding the neighbor accountable. If he is violating the law or abusing another person, or abusing us, we do him no favor by allowing such conduct to continue. As mentioned in chapter 9, there is a difference between not retaliating and allowing someone to treat you, or another person, without basic human decency. We cannot retaliate, but we can hold the person accountable and insist upon at least basic human decency and compliance with the law by the neighbor. Martin Luther King did not retaliate, but he insisted that blacks receive equal justice. By his stance he ultimately brought not only justice but goodwill as well.

We do not hold our neighbor accountable to get revenge any more than we hold our children accountable out of a desire to punish them. We hold them accountable because we want what is best for them, although it may be painful to them at the time. In Matthew 5:44 Jesus says that we must pray for the enemy that persecutes us. It will take sincere prayer on our part to insure that we are acting out of goodwill when we seek to hold our neighbor accountable without seeking revenge. Just as the role of a parent is difficult in determining when and how to hold a child accountable, it will often be difficult for us to know when and how to hold a neighbor accountable in the name of love. It is another reason why Jesus tells us to pray for our enemies. That prayer will help take away any bitterness toward the neighbor or a desire to retaliate against him.

There is a final point in this passage which requires explanation. After telling us that we are to love our enemies and pray for those who persecute us, as difficult as those are, Jesus winds up this passage by demanding something that is even more difficult: "Be perfect, therefore, as your heavenly Father is perfect." (Matt. 5:48) Given what Jesus said about recognizing the poverty of our spirit and the need to repent, how can he expect us to be perfect even as God is perfect? John Stott gives the best explanation of this passage:

> "Both the hunger for righteousness and the prayer for forgiveness, being continuous, are clear indications that Jesus did not expect his followers to become morally perfect in this life. The context shows that the 'perfection' he means relates to love, that perfect love of God which is shown even to those who do not return it. Indeed, scholars tell us that the Aramaic word which Jesus may well have used meant 'all-embracing'. The parallel verse in Luke's account of the Sermon confirms this: 'Be merciful, even as your Father is merciful. We are called to be perfect

in love, that is, to love even our enemies with the merciful, the inclusive love of God." (John Stott, *The Message of the Sermon on the Mount, p. 122,* Inter-Varsity Press)

In other words, by loving our neighbor as ourselves and praying for those who persecute us, we are behaving in the same fashion that our heavenly Father behaves towards both the righteous and the unrighteous. As we do this consistently, we will become perfect, not in the sense of our own moral perfection, but in the sense that we are becoming more like God. Remember, Jesus wants us to abide in him. As we abide in him his values become our values and we become more like him, not out of our own moral strength or goodness, but out of the strength and goodness of the one in whom we abide.

The core value is:

*"I will at all times strive to love my neighbor (including my enemies) as myself with the same love with which God has loved me."*

## *QUESTIONS TO CONSIDER*

1. Perhaps you were already aware that Jesus commanded his followers to love their enemies and pray for those who persecute them. If so, how well have you been doing this? Have you found it difficult to love those who dislike you? Have you found it difficult to pray for those who dislike you or mistreat you?

2. What has been the biggest impediment to your loving your enemies? What has been the biggest impediment to your praying for those who dislike or mistreat you? Has anger been part of the problem?

3. Before reading this chapter, what did you think that Jesus meant when he said you must love your enemies and pray for those who persecute you? Has your understanding of those commandments changed after reading this chapter? In what way? Give some

concrete examples of how you might show agape love to someone whom you dislike or consider an enemy.

4. Do you agree with the statement in this chapter "Whereas we may fall in love with our sweetheart, even if we did not intend to do so, we do not fall into agape love?" If you do not fall into agape love, what are some of the things you can do to enable you to love your enemies and your persecutors with agape love? Is this something that you think you have the capacity to do on your own? If not, how will you develop this capacity?

5. In this chapter we talked about holding another person accountable as part of agape love in the same way parents sometimes have to hold their children accountable. Can you give some examples of how you might be able to do this? How will you avoid slipping into a revenge mode?

6. In this chapter is a quote by John Stott regarding the meaning of Jesus' statement that we are to be perfect as our heavenly Father is perfect. Using your own words, explain how you will go about becoming "perfect." How quickly do you believe you will be able to do this?

7. What are the two or three things that you believe you must do to make loving your neighbor (including your enemies) a core value?

# CHAPTER 16

# TRUE GENEROSITY

*"Beware of practicing your piety before others in order to be seen by them; for then you have no reward from your Father in heaven. So whenever you give alms, do not sound a trumpet before you, as the hypocrites do in the synagogues and in the streets, so that they may be praised by others. Truly I tell you, they have received their reward. But when you give alms, do not let your left hand know what your right hand is doing, so that your alms may be done in secret; and your Father who sees in secret will reward you." (Matt. 6:1-4)*

This chapter is a natural sequel to the topic of Christian love which Jesus addressed in the previous chapter. Christian love does not exist in a vacuum. Our love for God, and our love for our fellow man, will be reflected in our actions. Indeed, remember that in chapter 1 we discussed that one's core values are determined by observing the person's *behavior,* not by what he or she says. There are certain things that a Christian is expected to do. Christians, like the Jews Jesus was addressing in the Sermon on the Mount, are expected to engage in almsgiving, prayer and fasting. Each of these Christian disciplines, when done appropriately, help us to develop and express our love for God in a tangible way. Jesus addresses the appropriate way to practice each of these three disciplines in the Sermon on Mount.

Jesus begins by saying "Beware of practicing your piety before others in order to be seen by them for then you have no reward from your

Father in heaven." (Matt. 6:1) The emphasis is and should be on *"in order to be seen by them."* These words of Jesus should not be surprising to us. Jesus wants us to abide in him. (John 15:4) We can only do that when we are obedient to him and to his commandments. If we perform some act of piety, such as almsgiving, prayer or fasting, to impress others or to gain their approval, we may obtain their approval but Jesus says that is the only approval or reward that we will get. Judging by the marketing strategies that most non-profit corporations use to raise money, that approval is apparently quite important. It is common for non-profit organizations not only to publicly announce the names of their donors, but to also announce the level of giving—such as announcing that a certain person has become a gold (or platinum or silver) donor for that charity. Even the church sometimes does this. Many churches have a wing of the church, a fellowship hall, or another facility named after a generous donor.

Jesus, however, instructs his disciples to avoid the practice of the "hypocrites" (the term often used by Jesus in reference to the Pharisees) who would go to great lengths to call attention to their almsgiving. The verbal picture Jesus drew was of a trumpeter blowing his trumpet to announce that the king, or some other high official, was about to pass by. However, this trumpet was being blown to call attention to the Pharisee who was about to give alms in a very public way. The Pharisee was about to get that which he craved the most—the attention and adulation of his peers, and others, who would admire him for being righteous.

So why is this so bad? Regardless of his motive, isn't the Pharisee doing a good thing by giving alms? Yes, he is. And Jesus says he will get his reward; however, that reward will come from men, not from God.

Why does Jesus come down so hard on the "hypocrites" or Pharisees? It is because the Pharisees were not acting out of love; they were acting out of self-interest and self-centeredness. They were interested not in how they could show the love of God, but rather in how they could gain the approval of their friends and colleagues. As Paul said in I

Corinthians 13:3, "If I give away all my possessions, and if I hand over my body so that I may boast, but do not have love, I gain nothing." Jesus said that such people are "hypocrites," which literally meant someone playing a role like a stage actor. That may win the approval of those whose approval the giver seeks, but it will not impress God. God wants us to be generous to one another just as he has been generous to us, and he wants our almsgiving to be the result of that generosity. One who is doing his acts of righteousness to be seen by friends and colleagues is not giving out of generosity but for recognition, and one who gives only if appropriate recognition is received has not yet developed a generous heart.

We might well question whether this focus on the motives in giving might not in itself become a distraction to us. Constantly questioning our own motives in giving a gift may just cause us to be more introspective and self-centered as a result of our giving. But Jesus has an amazingly simple solution to that problem. Just keep your gift a secret. By saying "do not let your left hand know what your right hand is doing," Jesus means that we should keep our gifts confidential—let it be just between you and God. And, in fact, we shouldn't even let ourselves be overly impressed with the almsgiving we have done. After all, we are just giving out of the abundance that God has given to us.

Jesus goes on to say that when we give in secret, God will see us in secret and he will reward us. Some people have a problem with the idea that Jesus says we will receive a reward for our generosity. They think that it is unspiritual to expect a reward. However, throughout the beatitudes, and the rest of the Sermon on the Mount, Jesus repeatedly tells us that we will receive a reward for being obedient. "Blessed are the merciful, *for they will receive mercy.*" "Blessed are the pure in heart, *for they will see God.*" "Blessed are the peacemakers, *for they will be called children of God.*" In each of Jesus' teachings there is an inherent reward in being obedient to him. None of the promised rewards are material rewards, but they are rewards nevertheless. Indeed, for those hungering and thirsting after righteousness, they are the rewards that best meet our needs.

Almsgiving is another area in which Jesus expects us to "seek first the kingdom of God." The person who gives without the expectation of recognition for giving is seeking first God's approval. Indeed, if he keeps his giving a secret God's approval is the only approval he is likely to receive. Jesus is saying that is as it should be. It is the best approval we could ever hope for.

The core value is:

*"I will be generous in giving to the poor, the needy and the afflicted and will avoid seeking any recognition for my giving."*

## QUESTIONS TO CONSIDER

1. What do you think is the problem with our doing good deeds and then letting others know that we have done those good deeds? What was the point Jesus was trying to make by using the verbal picture of a trumpeter blowing his horn before giving alms? Which of the beatitudes relates directly to this problem?

2. Do you think it would be difficult to keep your good deeds a secret? Do you think the real purpose of Jesus' admonition to keep our good deeds a secret is to insure that no one knows or to keep our focus on serving and being obedient to God?

3. Jesus said that when we give in secret, God sees us in secret and will reward us. Do you believe that you have received rewards for some of the good deeds that you have done? Give examples. Were these monetary rewards, or some other kind?

4. The title of this chapter is "True Generosity." What do you believe you can do to become a more generous person—of your time, your money and your talents?

5. Are you examining your behavior regularly to see whether you are being generous in giving to the poor, the needy and the afflicted? Has it become a core value for you? If not, what do you think you should do to help make generosity become a core value for you?

# CHAPTER 17

# PRAYER

*"And whenever you pray, do not be like the hypocrites; for they love to stand and pray in the synagogues and at the street corners, so that they may be seen by others. Truly I tell you, they have received their reward. But whenever you pray, go into your room and shut the door and pray to your Father who is in secret; and your Father who sees in secret will reward you."* (Matt. 6:5-6)

If you have been wondering during the previous chapters how you are ever going to be able to live the core values that Jesus taught, you will begin to get your answer in this chapter. The fact is that we simply cannot live as Jesus taught solely in our own power. We must have the guidance, the moral clarity, the courage, the insight and the power that comes from abiding in Jesus if we are to live the life that Jesus expects us to live as his followers. Apart from him, this would be impossible. And if we are to abide in him, we can only do so if we commune with him regularly in prayer.

In the previous chapters we discussed that we should examine our own lives during a time of prayer and meditation to see how our lives are matching up to the values we profess to believe in. In the chapter on being a peacemaker (chapter 9), the chapter on anger (chapter 11) and the chapter on retaliation (chapter 14) we acknowledged that Jesus' instruction was to pray for those who have wronged us, pray for those with whom we are angry and pray for those who are our enemies. He instructed us to pray because sincere prayer changes us. It takes away the anger, the bitterness, the desire to retaliate. Without prayer we are simply unable to will ourselves to do that which we know we should do, especially in difficult or trying times.

How important is it for us to pray regularly? Consider this. Jesus is the Son of God. Yet while he was here on earth in human form, Jesus had a regular, fervent, active prayer life. Before he chose the 12 disciples he spent the night in prayer. (Luke 6:12-13) After feeding the 5,000 he sent his disciples off and went up to the mountain to pray. (Mark 6:46) Luke tells us that as Jesus healed many people the crowds grew larger and Jesus "would withdraw to deserted places and pray." (Luke 5:15-16) And on the night before his crucifixion Jesus prayed for his disciples (John 17:1-26) and for strength for himself for the ordeal that lay ahead for him (Matt. 26:36-46). Jesus' entire life reflected the primacy of prayer in the life of one seeking to be obedient to God. If Jesus found it necessary to make prayer a central part of his life, how much more do we need a regular prayer life.

In the Sermon on the Mount, Jesus makes quite clear that just as we are not to give alms publicly to get the praise of men, we should not pray publicly to impress others with how righteous or how spiritual we are. The whole point of prayer is for us to commune directly with God, not to attempt to impress our friends  There is a role for public prayers in public worship, and Jesus was not condemning public prayer during times of public worship, but we are not to try to impress others with our prayers by making our prayers more public than necessary.

This admonition of Jesus may seem strange to us today because the problem in our time is not that we too often pray in public when we should be praying in private, but that we do not pray enough either in public or in private. We spend more time talking *about* praying than we do actually praying. How often have you said that you will keep someone in your prayers and then never actually pray for that person?

It is a common failure and shows that a commitment to an active, regular prayer life is too often not a core value for us.

Another reason that an active prayer life is not a core value for us is that we are often unsure of how to pray and unsure of whether we have anything worthwhile to say to God. In short, we think that prayer is only for *spiritual* people and is beyond our capabilities. If you believe that, I have good news for you. Just as a mother delights in listening to her infant child coo and babble words that mean nothing to anyone else, the Father desires that you come to him in prayer, no matter how awkward you may feel or how inarticulate you may think you are.

It is far beyond the scope of this book to teach you how to pray, and I would be attempting to teach something about which I have much to learn myself. However, I strongly recommend that you read, and reread, Richard Foster's book *Prayer: Finding the Heart's True Home*, Harper Collins. I have read the book at least four times and feel that I have only begun to scratch the surface of what prayer is all about. He begins with simple prayer, and goes on to describe the many different types of prayer that we all pray from time to time, perhaps without realizing what we are doing. *Prayer: Finding the Heart's True Home* will be a resource to which you will frequently return.

But an even better place to begin to learn to pray is from the words of Jesus himself. After telling his disciples not to pray as the hypocrites do—to be seen by men—he goes on to tell them how to pray.

"When you are praying, do not heap up empty phrases as the Gentiles do; for they think that they will be heard because of their many words. Do not be like them, for your Father knows what you need before you ask him.

Pray then in this way:

Our Father in heaven,
  hallowed be your name.
Your kingdom come.
  Your will be done,

on earth as it is in heaven.
Give us this day our daily bread.
and forgive us our debts,
as we also have forgiven our debtors.
And do not bring us to the time of trial,
but rescue us from the evil one."
(Matt. 7:7-13)

As Jesus' words reveal, God is not interested in empty phrases or many words. Furthermore, we are not informing God of something he does not already know. We need to keep our prayers simple, straightforward and honest. As Richard Foster explains:

"In Simple Prayer we bring ourselves before God just as we are, warts and all. Like children before a loving father, we open our hearts and make our requests. We do not try to sort things out, the good from the bad. We simply and unpretentiously share our concerns and make our petitions. We tell God, for example, how frustrated we are with the co-worker at the office or the neighbor down the street. We ask for food, favorable weather, and good health." Richard Foster, *Prayer: Finding the Heart's True Home, p. 9,* Harper Collins.

As we become increasingly candid and honest with the Lord in our prayers we will find it easier to abide in him. The frequency of our prayers will increase; it will be a relief to us to release in prayer the normal frustrations of life and the pain that we all feel from time to time. He will be our constant companion and friend, as well as our Lord and savior. This, too, is what it means to abide in him.

Jesus gave his disciples the Lord's prayer as a model for what our prayers should be. This prayer is too deep and too profound (while at the same time being quite simple) for us to study in depth here, but note that the themes of this prayer reflect the core values that Jesus taught in the Sermon on the Mount.

Verse 9. *"Our Father in heaven, hallowed be your name."* Our heavenly Father is holy at all times; we are not. The first beatitude says that we are blessed if we recognize the poverty of our spirit. We come to recognize the poverty of our spirit not compared to someone else, but compared to God. Reminding ourselves in prayer of God's holiness also reminds us of the poverty of our own spirit and draws us closer to him to forgive us and to replace the poverty of our spirit with his goodness and righteousness.

Verse 10. *"Your kingdom come. Your will be done, on earth as it is in heaven."* We ask that his will be done on earth rather than our own. Indeed we ask that his will be done on earth *as it is in heaven.* In other words, we ask that God's will be done perfectly here on earth. This prayer counters our normal desire to be self-centered, to live out the core value of the world: "I want what I want when I want it." Instead, we ask God that his will be done on earth and in our lives.

Verse 11. *"Give us this day our daily bread."* We acknowledge our dependence upon him for things temporal as well as spiritual. What is more temporal than asking for "our daily bread" —our needs for the day. Some people have the mistaken idea that we should not ask God for material things. But Jesus never condemned our asking God for the things we *need;* indeed, he encouraged it. God knows our needs even before we ask (Matt. 6:8), but he wants us to ask nevertheless, even as we expect our children to ask of us. This is part of abiding in Jesus.

Verse 12. *"And forgive us our debts, as we also have forgiven our debtors."* We acknowledge our sins and ask his forgiveness. This reminds us that we are blessed when we mourn over our sins, and that God will comfort us in our repentance. (See Matt. 5:4) This verse also reminds us that we are to forgive those who have sinned against us. (More about this in the next chapter). This is part of hungering and thirsting for righteousness.

Verse 13. *"And do not bring us to the time of trial, but rescue us from the evil one."* We ask God's deliverance from temptation and from the evil one. Part of our hungering and thirsting after righteousness and seeking to have a pure heart involves keeping ourselves from sin. We are not likely to do that in our own power. In this part of the prayer we ask our Father to strengthen us and deliver us from temptation to sin and from the power of sin in our lives. Only with God's strength that will come as we pray can we overcome our desire to retaliate, our desire to hold on to our anger rather than release it, and our desire that harm rather than good come to our enemies.

Thus, each time we pray the Lord's prayer we are reinforcing the core values that Jesus taught, those values that Jesus expects us to incorporate into our character as we abide in him. We should pray the Lord's prayer often and with a clear vision of our character being reformed and our spirit being refreshed.

As Richard Foster says, the key to the heart of God is prayer. (Id. at 2). Prayer is also the key to our abiding in Jesus and developing the core values that he taught.

The core value is:

*"I will pray regularly, following the example of Jesus."*

## QUESTIONS TO CONSIDER

1. How often do you pray? Is there a period of time each day that you set aside for prayer or do you tend to pray whenever you need to or when it is convenient? What do you think you should do to make prayer a bigger part of your life? What is the biggest impediment to your making prayer a bigger part of your life?

2. Do you agree with the statement in this chapter that apart from Jesus you will not be able to develop and live by the core values that Jesus taught in the Sermon on the Mount? Why do you believe that is true? Do you believe that sincere prayer changes us? Can you give examples of how you have changed as a result of your prayers?

3. Do you find that you often tell someone you will keep him or her in your prayers and then not pray for that person? Why does that happen?

4. Do you feel inadequate in trying to pray? Do you feel that you just don't know how to pray? If so, will you consider getting a copy of Richard Foster's book *Prayer: Finding the Heart's True Home* and read it?

5. How often do you pray the Lord's prayer? How often do you pray using the words of one of your favorite psalms? Try praying using the psalms and the Lord's prayer and then honestly evaluate whether it helps your prayer life. These prayers will help you focus on God and open your heart and mind to true communion with him. Will you commit to trying this daily for at least two weeks and then evaluate the results?

6. Do you agree that the Lord's prayer reminds us of the core values that Jesus set forth in the Sermon on the Mount? Does this make the Lord's prayer more meaningful to you?

7. As mentioned in this chapter, scripture tells us that Jesus had an active prayer life while he was on earth. Why do you think that Jesus needed to have such an active prayer life? What does this tell you about our need for a regular prayer life?

# CHAPTER 18

# FORGIVENESS

*"And forgive us our debts, as we also have forgiven our debtors. . . . For if you forgive others their trespasses, your heavenly Father will also forgive you; but if you do not forgive others, neither will your Father forgive your trespasses." (Matt. 6:12, 14-15)*

These verses are some of the most frightening verses of scripture, and yet are reassuring at the same time. They are frightening because Jesus actually says that if we do not forgive others God will not forgive us. We expect, indeed, we depend upon God to forgive us. In chapter 3 we addressed the fact that we must acknowledge the poverty of our own spirit. In other words, we must come to acknowledge that we are sinners, having a sinful nature and separated from God. But we don't come to that realization to stay in that state. Once we recognize the poverty of our spirit we want forgiveness and reconciliation with God so that we can live in peace and harmony with him. That peace comes through Jesus Christ. As the Apostle Paul so beautifully said:

"So he came and proclaimed peace to you who were far off (Gentiles) and peace to those who were near (Jews); for through him both of us have access in one Spirit to the Father. So then you are no longer strangers and aliens, but you are citizens with the saints and also members of the household of God, built upon the foundation of the apostles and prophets, with Christ Jesus himself as the cornerstone." (Eph. 2: 17-20)

This forgiveness and reconciliation leads us into a new life that is different from the old life. In the Sermon on the Mount Jesus teaches us what this new life is like and how we are to live out this new life. We must allow God to change our character to conform to his character; his values must become our values; and his purposes must become our purposes. Just as our Father is ready to forgive us, we must also be ready to forgive those who trespass against us. Indeed, Jesus says that if we don't forgive those who have wronged us, neither will our Father forgive us.

In chapter 7 we examined Jesus' words that the merciful will be shown mercy, and concluded that those unwilling to show mercy will not receive mercy. The same pattern holds here. God is ready to forgive, but requires of us that we also be ready to forgive. And to the extent we are unwilling to forgive, to that same extent we will not receive forgiveness. Jesus was quite explicit with his disciples about this point. "And if the same person sins against you seven times a day, and turns back to you seven times and says, 'I repent,' you must forgive." (Luke 17: 4)

Jesus also specifically addressed the requirement to forgive in the parable of the unforgiving servant (Matt. 18: 23-34). There was a king who wanted to settle accounts with his slaves and called to him first one who owed him ten thousand talents. When the slave could not pay the amount owed, the king ordered that the slave, his wife and his children be sold, together with all his possessions, to pay the amount owed. But the slave begged the king for patience and promised to repay all he owed. Out of pity, rather than grant more time the king graciously forgave the entire debt. The same slave, however, shortly thereafter came upon a fellow slave who owed him a much smaller amount and "seizing him by the throat" insisted that the fellow slave pay him all that he owed. The fellow slave fell down and begged for more time to pay but the slave refused and had the fellow slave thrown into prison. When word of this got back to the king he summoned the slave and said to him "You wicked slave! I forgave you all that debt because you pleaded with me. Should you not have had mercy on your fellow slave, as I had mercy on you?" The king then handed the slave over to prison and torture until the slave had paid the entire debt.

Jesus' chilling words to his disciples about how this parable applies to them (and to us) should focus our attention on forgiveness being of paramount importance: "So my heavenly Father will also do to every one of you, if you do not forgive your brother or sister from your heart." (Matt. 18: 35) Clearly, forgiveness of others is at the core of the life Jesus expects us to live.

The importance of our forgiving others is incorporated into the very fabric of the Lord's prayer. Jesus taught us to pray "And forgive us our debts, as we also have forgiven our debtors." Unfortunately, we often say these words without giving a passing thought to the meaning of what we are saying. We are, in fact, asking God *not* to forgive us if we do not forgive those who trespass against us—a remarkable thing for us to ask of God. Why would Jesus include such a statement in the Lord's prayer, knowing us as he does? In my opinion, Jesus included it to remind us how important it is for us to forgive. Our own forgiveness depends upon our willingness to forgive others. In what other way could we be so often reminded that we must forgive, and how important it is that we do forgive?

Once we see what great importance Jesus puts on our willingness to forgive, we understand more fully why Jesus addressed anger before he addressed forgiveness. We cannot forgive someone while retaining our anger against that person. And if we cannot release that anger and forgive the person who has sinned against us, Jesus says that we "will be liable to the hell of fire." (Matt. 5: 22) By refusing to forgive, thereby blocking our own forgiveness, we create a hell for ourselves here on earth.

But God has better plans for us. As the author of Hebrews points out:

"And the Holy Spirit also testifies to us, for after saying, 'This is the covenant that I will make with them after those days, says the Lord: I will put my laws in their hearts, and I will write them on their minds,' he also adds, 'I will remember their sins and their lawless deeds no more.'" (Heb. 10:15-17)

In other words, God will change us in our heart, at the core of our being, so that we will forgive just as God has forgiven us. God will remember our sins no more, and he expects us to remember no more the trespasses against us.

At the beginning of this chapter I said that Jesus words are frightening, but also reassuring. It is reassuring that Jesus believes not only that we *can* change but that if we abide in him we *will* change. The ability and willingness to forgive is one of the critical core values that we must have to live the Christian life. It is comforting to know that Jesus believes that if we abide in him forgiveness will become a core value for us.

The core value is:

*"I will promptly forgive all offenses against me, just as God has forgiven me."*

## QUESTIONS TO CONSIDER

1. Forgiveness is at the heart of our relationship with God. Describe how you first came to realize that God had forgiven your sins. How did you respond to that realization that you were forgiven? How did you feel upon realizing that your sins had been forgiven?

2. What was your reaction the first time that you learned, perhaps from reading the scriptures quoted in this chapter, that God expects you to forgive others who have sinned against you? What was your reaction when you learned that if you are unwilling to forgive others, God will not forgive you of your sins?

3. Do you think that your character can ever become like the character of Jesus without your learning to promptly forgive all offenses against you? What is the major impediment to your forgiving other people?

4.  Have you ever acted like the slave in the parable of the unforgiving servant who refused to forgive his fellow slave? What were the circumstances? What can you do to get to the point of being more ready to forgive?

5.  Have you ever considered the words of the Lord's prayer before regarding your asking God to forgive you according to the measure by which you forgive? Do you find that frightening? What role do you think anger plays in your unwillingness to forgive?

6.  The core value for this chapter is "I will promptly forgive all offenses against me . . . ." Is this an act of the will, or is it an act of the heart (involving the emotions)? If it is primarily an act of the will, can you forgive even when you don't particularly feel like forgiving? Is this an act of agape love that we discussed in chapter 15?

# CHAPTER 19

# MONEY: MASTER OR SERVANT?

*"No one can serve two masters; for a slave will either hate the one and love the other, or be devoted to the one and despise the other. You cannot serve God and wealth." (Matt. 6:24)*

No discussion about core values for the Christian is complete without addressing the issue of money. It is a topic that Jesus never shirked from addressing; in fact, he spoke more about money and wealth, and their dangers, than he did about prayer. Undoubtedly, it is because Jesus understood the power that a desire for wealth or possessions can have over a person, even one who professes to be his disciple. The danger is that the desire to obtain or maintain wealth, or lifestyle, or certain possessions can warp our priorities to the point we are no longer hungering and thirsting after righteousness but rather for material possessions. It is a danger that lurks for each of us. We should never assume that just because we have professed our faith in Jesus Christ that we will somehow be immune from an unhealthy desire for wealth and material possessions.

Jesus' teaching about money is most direct in his encounter with a rich young man who came to Jesus and asked "What must I do to inherit eternal life?" (Mark 10:17-22) Jesus responded that he must keep the commandments. The rich young man responded that he had done so.

And he must have been sincere in his answer, for Mark tells us that Jesus "loved him." But Jesus, knowing that the young man had not yet given God first priority in his life, told him "You lack one thing; go, sell what you own, and give the money to the poor, and you will have treasure in heaven; then come, follow me." At this point, the rich young man was faced with the one issue that was preventing him from being a faithful disciple: his love of his wealth. This must have been the first time this young man had considered that his wealth was a barrier to his relationship with God, for Mark tells us that "he was shocked." Mark also tells us that he "went away grieving, for he had many possessions." When faced with the choice of having his relationship with God or having his money, he chose the money.

The rich young man was not the only one shocked that day. Mark tells us that Jesus then looked at his disciples and said "Children, how hard it is to enter the kingdom of God! It is easier for a camel to go through the eye of a needle than for someone who is rich to enter the kingdom of God." Mark also tells us that Jesus' disciples were "greatly astounded" and asked "Then who can be saved?" (Mark 10:24-26)

So, what is it about money or wealth that caused Jesus to give such a warning to the rich? Are we endangering our very salvation simply by having possessions or even some wealth (and we should keep in mind that even in these difficult economic times the average American lives a lifestyle that can only be described as rich by much of the world)? No, Jesus is not condemning your having possessions or wealth; he is condemning your letting your possessions or wealth have you.

In chapter 1 and in subsequent chapters we discussed that our default core value, if not replaced by the core values that Jesus taught, is self-centeredness. We want what we want when we want it. And what we often want is a lifestyle full of luxuries and possessions that far exceed our needs. Why is there so much interest in celebrities in our culture? At least part of the answer is that they usually live lavish lifestyles characterized by wealth, possessions and independence that we can scarcely imagine. And it is not just the material possessions alone that capture our imagination; it is also the power that great wealth gives them, that sets them apart from the life that the rest of us live, and that seems to make them immune to concerns about what other people think of them.

Do not underestimate how strong the temptation is to put our hope or our trust in material possessions to bring us happiness and fulfillment. It is instructive that one of the temptations that Satan put before Jesus when Jesus was tempted in the wilderness—indeed, it was the final temptation—was the offer to give Jesus all the kingdoms of the world. Listen carefully to the offer with which Jesus was tempted:

> "Again, the devil took him to a very high mountain and showed him all the kingdoms of the world and their splendor; and he said to him, 'All these I will give you, if you will fall down and worship me.'" (Matt. 4:8-9)

If Satan believed that he could tempt even Jesus with worldly power and possessions, we can know with a high degree of certainty that we will also be tempted in the realm of money, possessions and the power that money and possessions can bring.

At this point some of you may be thinking that this is not and will not be a temptation to you because you have little money and few possessions. Unfortunately, human nature does not change just because you have little wealth. It is just as possible for a poor person to become obsessed with material possessions as it is a wealthy person. The rich man may covet a new Bentley, whereas the poor man may covet a used Honda, but covetousness is covetousness regardless of the object of the covetousness. Furthermore, the rich man, though he may cling to his riches, has already learned that wealth does not automatically bring peace and happiness, whereas the poor man is still assuming that peace and happiness will be his if only he can win the lottery, be the beneficiary of the estate of some distant relative, or otherwise come into considerable wealth.

In the Lord's prayer Jesus gave us the model of asking God to meet our needs (our "daily bread"). In the next chapter, we will see that Jesus told his disciples not to worry about what we will eat, what we will drink, or what we will wear because God knows we need those things and he will provide. To have our needs met we need a certain amount of money, so the money itself is not evil. As Paul said, it is the *"love* of money" that is the root of all kinds of evil. (I Tim. 6:10) Once we become a lover of money and possessions, money is no longer our servant that can make our lives happier and enable us to help others; it becomes our master. As Ecclesiastes tells us "The lover of money will not be satisfied with money; nor the lover of wealth, with gain." (Eccl. 5:10) In other words, once you become a lover of money you will never be satisfied; you will never have enough. Compare that with the words of Jesus: "Blessed are those who hunger and thirst for righteousness, for they will be filled." (Matt. 5:6) To simplify, devote your life to money and you will never have enough of that which you want the most; devote your life to God by hungering and thirsting for a right relationship with him and you will be filled with that which you want the most. It is a clear choice that each person must make.

In the Sermon on the Mount Jesus candidly tells us we simply cannot serve God and wealth. It is like a slave trying to serve two masters. A slave only had one master, his owner, and that is who he served. A slave could not have two masters. If someone should foolishly try to cause a slave to have two masters it would not work. He would be devoted to one or the other, but not both. Likewise, we cannot devote ourselves to God and to wealth. Only one of those can be our master. We may think that we can maintain our primary devotion to God while also devoting ourselves to building wealth at the same time. But like the rich young man who approached Jesus, we may find that our primary devotion has shifted from God to our wealth. The reason that Charles Browne got into trouble is that the desire to have the possessions and lifestyle that he wanted for himself and his wife became stronger than his desire to be obedient to Jesus. He may have thought that he was still serving the Lord, but he learned, too late, that the one real master he was serving was his desire for wealth and possessions.

Is Jesus saying that it is wrong to have wealth or to work hard and, perhaps, thereby accumulate some wealth? No, Jesus is simply telling us that we must "strive first for the kingdom of God and his righteousness" (Matt. 6:33) and give him our first priority at all times. If we do that, money will be our servant that will bless us and those with whom we share our wealth. But if we do not give God first priority in our life, money will quickly become our first priority as we revert to a self-centered life. Even the most faithful among us must pray daily that we will, with God's help, overcome this temptation.

The core value is:

*"I will always insure that money is my servant and not my master."*

## QUESTIONS TO CONSIDER

1. What we do with our money is one of the best indicators of what our priorities are. What do your spending habits say about what is most important in your life?

2. Try to put yourself in the shoes of the rich young man that came to Jesus and asked "What must I do to inherit eternal life?" If Jesus told you to go, sell what you own, give the money to the poor, and follow him, how do you think you would respond? Why do you think you would respond that way? What does that say about your priorities?

3. How do you think you can tell whether money and possessions are your servant or your master? How do you think you can tell whether you have your money and your possessions or whether they have you?

4.  Are you fascinated by celebrities or by extremely wealthy people? What is it about them that makes them so fascinating? Are there wealthy people that you know personally whose lifestyle or possessions you envy? If you could be in their situation how do you think your life would be different? Would that help you give God first priority in your life or would it hinder it?

5.  Were you surprised to learn that one of the temptations Satan used on Jesus was the temptation to have great wealth and possessions? Why do you think Satan would use this temptation on Jesus? Is the desire for wealth and possessions a typical human desire?

6.  Do you agree with the statement in this chapter that "It is just as possible for a poor person to become obsessed with material possessions as it is a wealthy person?" If so, why do you agree? Is it based on your observation of people? If you disagree, what is the reason for your disagreement?

7.  Do you agree with the statement in this chapter that "once you become a lover of money you will never be satisfied; you will never have enough." What is the basis for your agreement or disagreement?

8.  Do you agree with Jesus' statement that we cannot serve God and wealth? That it is like a slave trying to serve two masters? If so, what do you believe that you need to do to insure that your only master is Jesus and not wealth or possessions? How does this relate to giving God first priority in our lives?

# CHAPTER 20

# TRUST AND DO NOT WORRY

*"Therefore I tell you, do not worry about your life, what you will eat or what you will drink, or about your body, what you will wear. Is not life more than food, and the body more than clothing? . . . . and indeed your heavenly Father knows that you need all these things. But strive first for the kingdom of God and his righteousness, and all these things will be given to you as well." (Matt. 6: 25, 32-33)*

In the previous chapter we discussed how the desire for wealth or possessions could easily become our master and divert us from making our relationship with God our first priority. Sometimes our focus on wealth or possessions arises not out of greed but out of fear—the fear that we may lose what we have, or that we may not have enough to meet our needs, or at least what we think we need. Knowing men and women as he does, Jesus immediately follows his warning about letting wealth become our master with reassuring words that our needs will be met.

Worry, of course, comes from fear. It is not fear of what is happening now, but of what we think may or may not happen in the future. Will I have enough to eat? Will I have sufficient clothes to wear? Today, we might add: Will I get into college, or at least the college I want? Will I lose my job? Will I be able to pay my mortgage or my rent? The things to worry about in life are endless because our fears about the future can be endless.

Note that Jesus does not say that the things about which we worry are unimportant. Usually, we worry about things because they *are* important. If a father or mother loses a job, the whole family may suffer; if a family's mortgage is foreclosed the whole family may be homeless. No, Jesus does not say these things are unimportant. To the contrary, he said "indeed your heavenly Father knows that you need all these things." (Matt. 6:32) The point that Jesus is making is that we do not have to go through life full of fear, worrying about whether our basic needs in life will be met. He wants us to get to the point that we can go through life overcoming our fears and living without worry. He wants us to live as the psalmist described:

> "Therefore we will not fear, though the earth should change, though the mountains shake in the heart of the sea; though its waters roar and foam, though the mountains tremble with its tumult." (Psalm 46: 2-3)

Living without worry can be an extremely liberating experience. Who has not felt the tightness in his temples and the foreboding feeling in his chest that something unpleasant if not horrible may happen? Living with worry and fear robs us of our joy in life and detracts us from living in a close relationship with the Lord. Who among us does not want to live without worry and fear? But how do we do it? How do we come to the point that though fears and worries may arise, they do not control us or rob us of the peace and joy that God wishes for us?

Jesus had a surprising, but highly effective, answer. He said we must come to him like a little child. (Matt 18: 2-3) He is not saying that we must become *childish* but rather we must have the trust of a child. He is pointing out that a little child does not worry about whether he will have enough to eat or to wear; he trusts his parents for these things. A little child does not get ulcers from worry; she is secure in the presence of her parents. In other words, the relationship between the child and the parents is one of trust. The child does not worry about what may happen because the parents are there and the child trusts the parents.

Jesus is telling us in the Sermon on the Mount that we should put our trust in God, knowing that he both knows and intends to meet our needs. Therefore, we have no reason to live in fear, or worry about what the future may bring. Jesus' words should bring us comfort and enable us to live freely in the present, unencumbered by a fear of the future.

> "Therefore I tell you, do not worry about your life, what you will eat or what you will drink, or about your body, what you will wear. Is not life more than food, and the body more than clothing? Look at the birds of the air; they neither sow nor reap nor gather into barns, and yet your heavenly Father feeds them. Are you not of more value than they? And can any of you by worrying add a single hour to your span of life? And why do you worry about clothing? Consider the lilies of the field, how they grow; they neither toil nor spin, yet I tell you, even Solomon in all his glory was not clothed like one of these. But if God so clothes the grass of the field, which is alive today and tomorrow is thrown into the oven, will he not much more clothe you—you of little faith? Therefore do not worry, saying 'What will we eat?' or 'What will we drink?' or 'What will we wear?' For it is the gentiles who strive for all these things; and indeed your heavenly Father knows that you need all these things. But strive first for the kingdom of God and his righteousness, and all these things will be given to you as well. So do not worry about tomorrow, for tomorrow will bring worries of its own. Today's trouble is enough for today." (Matt. 6: 25-34)

To the extent our trust in the Lord grows, our fears and worries about the future will subside. We will find ourselves living more in the present because although we don't know what the future may bring, we trust that God will be there in the future with us. As with most other things in the Christian life, this will not happen immediately and will not be easy. We should recognize that our natural inclination is to be independent and self-reliant rather than put our total trust in another, even if that other is God himself. But one of the primary reasons that we became a Christian in the first place is be able to spend eternity with the Lord. If we trust God for our eternal salvation, shouldn't we also trust him in this life?

God wants us to trust him. Listen to the comforting words that God gave to the people of Israel in the midst of their captivity in Babylon to encourage them to trust him for deliverance from their captivity.

> "For surely I know the plans I have for you, says the Lord, plans for your welfare and not for harm, to give you a future with hope. Then when you call upon me and come and pray to me, I will hear you. When you search for me, you will find me." (Jer. 29: 11-12)

One sure way to increase our trust in God is to have an active prayer life. As we observed in chapter 17, Jesus had an active prayer life, and he trusted the Father completely. As you pray, keep a journal of your prayer requests and a record of all of the answers to your prayers. As you review the record of your requests to God and how often God has answered, your trust in God will grow. It will become easier to trust God for the little things in life as well as the big things. In the Sermon on the Mount Jesus boldly says that if we strive first for the kingdom of God, all of our needs will be met by the Father.

One word of caution, however. Although Jesus says that the Father will meet our needs, he does not say that we will not have to work. In fact, in the parable of the talents (Matt. 25:14-30) Jesus praised the servants who worked hard and invested the talents (a unit of money) the master gave them and rebuked the servant who did nothing but dig a hole in the ground and bury the one talent he was given. The servant who did not work received the master's wrath rather than his approval. The Apostle Paul stated this same principle to the early church slightly differently in saying: "Anyone unwilling to work should not eat." (II Thess. 3:10) Thus, the promise that our needs will be met—and that we should therefore not worry—should never cause us to be lazy or unwilling to work.

There is another way that your trust in the Lord will grow. Through the Sermon on the Mount, Jesus laid out for his followers the core values they should live by. At the conclusion of the sermon Jesus said that "Everyone then who hears these words of mine and acts on them will be like a wise man who built his house on rock." (Matt. 7:24) If you earnestly and sincerely try living by the core values addressed in this book, you will find that your life will be changed. Hopefully, you have already begun the process of adopting these core values and regularly holding yourself accountable before God for your actions. If you have done so, you probably have already begun to see the transforming effect these core values can have on your life. If you continue to be faithful in living by these core values you will continue to see meaningful change, and as you see that change your trust in God will grow. You will also notice that your worries and fears no longer control you. With the psalmist you will be able to say:

"Even though I walk through the darkest valley, I fear no evil; for you are with me; your rod and your staff—they comfort me." (Psalm 23:4)

The core value is:

*"I will seek to overcome my fears and worries by placing my trust in God; I will make all decisions in life trusting him."*

## QUESTIONS TO CONSIDER

1. Is worry a problem for you? What do you worry about the most? Why do you think you worry about these particular things? Is trust a problem for you? If so, why do you believe you have trouble trusting people? Why do you have trouble trusting God?

2. Did you worry as a child? Do you recall worrying while your parents were around? Why do you think you did not worry (or not worry as much) when your parents were around? Do you think you can develop the same level of trust in God that you had in your parent when you were a child? How might you do that?

3. Would you like to get to the point in life that you are able to over-come all of your fears? Do you think that developing the core values that we have been studying in this book will help get you to that point? Why do you think developing these core values will help you overcome your fears?

4. Do you really believe that God wants to meet your needs? Do you think you can get to the point that you trust God to meet your needs? Do you think you have a realistic view of what your true needs are? Is some of your worry about your wants rather than your needs?

5. Have you addressed your worries with God in prayer? Do you think you have been honest with God about your worries? Have you considered keeping a prayer log of your prayer requests, including your worries and fears, and tracking how God responds to those prayers? If you have done that have you found that most of your prayers have been answered? Has that increased your trust in God?

6. If you can imagine living without fear, or promptly overcoming your fears when they arise, what do you believe your life would be like? How would it be different than it is now? Do you believe that God wants you to get to that point in life? If so, what does that say about your current level of trust in God? How do you think you can come to trust God more?

# CHAPTER 21

# BEING JUDGMENTAL

*"Do not judge, so that you may not be judged. For with the judgment you make you will be judged, and the measure you give will be the measure you get. Why do you see the speck in your neighbor's eye, but do not notice the log in your own eye? Or how can you say to your neighbor, 'Let me take the speck out of your eye,' while the log is in your own eye? You hypocrite, first take the log out of your own eye, and then you will see clearly to take the speck out of your neighbor's eye." (Matt. 7: 1-5)*

These verses include some of the strongest admonitions of Jesus to his followers. They are also some of the most often quoted by those who are not Christian. They are quick to say to the Christian that he has no right to judge the unbeliever or to declare that what the unbeliever is doing is wrong. Additionally, many people today contend that a Christian should not engage in public debate on moral issues if his or her position is based upon religious beliefs. To do so, they contend, is to attempt to force our religious views on others, and, besides, even Jesus said we should not judge. So, how do we "let our light (as a Christian) shine before others" (Matt. 5:16) without standing in judgment of those whose actions or beliefs we believe are contrary to what Jesus taught? And what did Jesus mean when he said "Do not judge, so that you may not be judged"?

To find an answer to these questions we must go back to the first beatitude. In chapter 3 we discussed that we are all sinners, and we must

143

come to recognize the poverty of our spirit. When we do so we realize that we all stand before God as sinners in need of his mercy and forgiveness. Therefore, we have no grounds to feel superior to anyone else, even those who may be greater sinners at the moment than we are. God alone is the judge of each of us, and he has not delegated to us the right to stand in judgment of a fellow sinner. Even Jesus said that he did not come to judge. "Indeed, God did not send the Son into the world to condemn (judge) the world, but in order that the world might be saved through him." (John 3:17)

Not only did Jesus tell us that we are not to act as judge of another, but that if we do judge another we will judged by the same measure or standard that we use. This should sound familiar to you. In chapter 7 we learned that if we are merciful we will receive mercy, and if we are not, we will not receive mercy. In chapter 18, we saw that if we do not forgive others their sins, God will not forgive us our sins. In each of those instances, Jesus pointed out that we will receive back that which we first give. If we give mercy, we receive mercy. If we give forgiveness, we receive forgiveness. Here, Jesus is saying that if we stand in judgment of another person we will be judged by the same standard by which we have judged our neighbor (remember that in God's eyes everyone is our neighbor). We, of course, judge our neighbor because of his particular sin. But even if we do not have the same sin as the person we are judging—and we should remember that we are often most critical of those who have the same sins that we do—we will still be judged by the same standard for the sins which we *do* have.

Furthermore, if we presume to be a judge, we are claiming that we know the law, for a judge is responsible for knowing the law. Therefore, we can hardly claim ignorance when our own sins are judged. Jesus is telling us to look honestly at ourselves. When we do so we will recognize that our own sins are sufficient to disqualify us to sit in judgment of another person. In chapter 5, we examined Jesus' admonition that we should be humble. Humility comes from seeing ourselves as we truly are, particularly when compared to a holy God. When we are truly humble we will recognize that we are not qualified to be a judge of anyone else. Only God is qualified to do that. As the Apostle Paul said:

"Why do you pass judgment on your brother or sister? Or why do you despise your brother or sister? For we will all stand before the judgment seat of God." (Rom. 14:10)

John Stott has perhaps best described the problem of our setting ourselves up as a judge. He calls it "censoriousness."

"Censoriousness is a compound sin consisting of several unpleasant ingredients. It does not mean to assess people critically, but to judge them harshly. The censorious critic is a fault-finder who is negative and destructive towards other people and enjoys actively seeking out their failings. He puts the worst possible construction on their motives, pours cold water on their schemes and is ungenerous towards their mistakes.

Worse than that, to be censorious is to set oneself up as a censor, and so to claim the competence and authority to sit in judgment upon one's fellow men. But if I do this, I am casting both myself and my fellows in the wrong role. Since when have they been my servants, responsible to me? And since when have I been their lord and judge?" (John Stott, *The Message of the Sermon on the Mount, p.176,* Inter-Varsity Press)

If we agree that we should not and do not have the right to judge another person does that mean that we cannot declare that what someone is doing is wrong? Are we simply to remain silent, even among our own family and friends, as to whether someone's actions are right or wrong, or even harmful? Are we to adopt the standard of the world to "live and let live" regardless of the consequences?

These questions are readily answered by considering how biblical characters dealt with the question of whether someone's actions were right or wrong. John the Baptist, whose ministry was to proclaim the coming of the Messiah, pulled no punches with those to whom he spoke:

"John said to the crowds that came out to be baptized by him, 'You brood of vipers! Who warned you to flee from the wrath to come? Bear fruits worthy of repentance. Do not begin to say to yourselves 'We have Abraham as our ancestor'; for I tell you, God is able from these stones to raise up children to Abraham. Even now the ax is lying at the root of the trees; every tree therefore that does not bear good fruit is cut down and thrown into the fire.'" (Luke 3: 7-9)

Clearly, John was not hesitant to discern whether the actions of those who came to him were right or wrong, good or evil.

Consider also the words of Jesus, especially to the scribes and Pharisees, the religious leaders of his day:

"Woe to you, scribes and Pharisees, hypocrites! For you tithe mint, dill, and cummin, and have neglected the weightier matters of the law: justice and mercy and faith. It is these you ought to have practiced without neglecting the others. You blind guides! You strain out a gnat but swallow a camel!" (Matt. 23:23-24)

When the Pharisees tried to trap Jesus in the crossfire of one of the most contentious issues of the time regarding whether a Jew should pay taxes to Caesar, Jesus was quick to point out the hypocrisy of his questioners:

"'Why are you putting me to the test, you hypocrites? Show me the coin used for the tax.' And they brought him a denarius. Then he said to them, 'Whose head is this and whose title?' They answered, 'The emperor's.' Then he said to them, 'Give therefore to the emperor the things that are the emperor's, and to God the things that are God's.'" (Matt. 22:18-21)

And when the scribes and Pharisees asked Jesus why his disciples broke the traditions of the elders, such as failing to ceremoniously wash their hands before they ate, Jesus left no doubt that their teaching missed the mark of what God intended:

"He answered them, 'And why do you break the commandment of God for the sake of your tradition? For God said, 'Honor your father and your mother,' and 'whoever speaks evil of father or mother must surely die.' But you say that whoever tells father or mother, 'Whatever support you might have had from me is given to God,' then that person need not honor the father. So, for the sake of your tradition, you make void the word of God. You hypocrites! Isaiah prophesied rightly about you when he said: 'This people honors me with their lips, but their hearts are far from me; in vain do they worship me, teaching human precepts as doctrines.'" (Matt. 15:3-9)

In each of the instances above, Jesus or John boldly spoke out regarding what was right and what was wrong, what was good and what was evil. Note, however, that John and Jesus were able to speak out so forcefully about right and wrong and good and evil because their lives were consistent with what they were saying. In other words, their core values and their actions were consistent; they were not hypocrites, as were those whom they reprimanded.

The early church put a premium on the Christian discerning what was within the will of God, and what was not. That was not always easy for the new gentile Christians who were often living in decadent cities whose culture was strongly at odds with the standards of behavior that Jesus demanded of his followers. To these early Christians Paul said, "Do not be conformed to this world, but be transformed by the renewing of your minds, *so that you may discern what is the will of God—what is good and acceptable and perfect.*" (Rom. 12:2) But to the same Roman Christians Paul also said "Why do you pass judgment on your brother or sister? . . . For we will all stand before the judgment seat of God." (Rom. 14:10) So the early church followed the teaching of Christ: Do not judge other people, but discern whether what they are doing is right or wrong.

If we are to live out the core values that Jesus taught, we must discern first whether our own actions are consistent with Jesus' values. As Jesus said, "first take the log out of your own eye, and then you will see clearly to take the speck out of your neighbor's eye." (Matt. 7:5) As we get the log out of our own eye we will see the actions of our neighbors more clearly, not to judge them, but to show them compassion and the agape love that God has so richly shown us.

If we follow the example of Jesus we should never be afraid to speak out for what is good and what is right and to stand against what is evil and what is harmful. And that is as true for public issues and public debate as it is in our personal relationships. As Christians, we should never allow anyone to ban us from the public square simply because we espouse moral values based upon the teaching of the one we worship. We have a constitutional right to express our values, and the world needs the values that Jesus taught now more than ever.

The core value is:

*"I will stand in judgment of no one, but I will always try to discern good and evil based upon Jesus' commandments."*

## QUESTIONS TO CONSIDER

1. Have you ever felt that someone was judging you? How did you react to that? How receptive were you to the judgment that was being passed on you?

2. Have you ever judged someone else? What was the reason for your judging that person? How did that person react? How do you think you would fare if you were judged by the same standard by which you judged the other person?

3. John Stott is quoted in this chapter as calling our tendency to judge another person as "censoriousness." Do you know anyone that you think is "censorious?" How does that manifest itself? Do you think

that you have ever been "censorious?" If so, how do you intend to avoid being censorious in the future?

4. Although we are not to judge other people, we must still discern between right and wrong, between good and evil. How can you make decisions between right and wrong and between good and evil without being judgmental? Are you able to love the sinner but not the sin? How do you think you can learn to do this?

5. Have you ever been criticized for being judgmental or for attempting to force your religious beliefs on others when you spoke out publicly about some moral or political issue? You have the constitutionally protected right to speak out on public issues. What is there about being a Christian that would cause you to forfeit that right? Do you think that as a Christian God expects you to speak out on moral issues? Do you think that you can do this without being judgmental?

# CHAPTER 22

# THE LIFE OF FAITH

*"Ask, and it will be given you; search, and you will find; knock, and the door will be opened for you. For everyone who asks receives, and everyone who searches finds, and for everyone who knocks, the door will be opened. Is there anyone among you who, if your child asks for bread, will give a stone? Or if the child asks for a fish, will give a snake? If you then, who are evil, know how to give good gifts to your children, how much more will your father in heaven give good things to those who ask him! In everything do to others as you would have them do to you; for this is the law and the prophets."*

Throughout this book I have said that if you learn to live by the core values that Jesus taught, your life will change. It will change from what it was—a life that was largely self-centered rather than God-centered— to a life lived in harmony and fellowship with God. This chapter should help you see just how different God wants your life to be.

Many people are turned off by the thought of making any kind of Christian commitment because they believe that they will be compelled to follow a long list of rules and prohibitions. They believe that the Christian life would be dull and without excitement. They also doubt that we can really have an intimate relationship with a benevolent God that earnestly desires to fellowship with us. If you have had some of those thoughts yourself, you should consider seriously the words of Jesus quoted above.

Imagine what living like this would be.

Jesus tells us to ask of the Father, and he follows that with a promise: "it will be given to you." In the Lord's prayer Jesus taught us to ask that God's will be done on earth ("Thy kingdom come, thy will be done."); he taught us to ask for our "daily bread", which refers not just to food but to all our daily needs. He taught us to ask for forgiveness of our sins and for deliverance from temptation. Here, Jesus goes even further, and tells us simply to ask, believing in faith that for whatever we ask, we will receive.

Does this mean that I can ask for *anything* that I want and God will give it to me? No; to expect that is to turn God into a cosmic Santa Clause who gives us whatever is on our Christmas list simply because we want it. To receive what we ask for, we must ask while living out the core values that Jesus taught, which means that we must ask in accordance with God's will ("Thy will be done on earth as it is in heaven."). Furthermore, the promise that "it will be given you" does not necessarily mean that we will receive precisely what we ask for. But Jesus promises that God will respond to our requests. I am very thankful that God has not granted me every request that I have ever made of him. He has known far better than I what requests to grant, what requests to deny, and what requests to grant at a later time.

The point Jesus is making however, is that *God wants us to ask*. He wants us to live in such an intimate relationship with him that we will trust him with all our requests, confident that he wants what is best for us. Furthermore, Jesus points out that even though we are sinful, unlike God, we know how to give good gifts to our children. If a child asks his father for bread, the father isn't going to give the child something that may look like bread, but cannot be eaten; if he asks for a fish, the father isn't going to give him a snake instead. If we, with all our faults, can be relied upon to be generous and helpful to our children, how much more can we rely upon our heavenly Father to be generous and helpful to us. Of course, just as a parent must sometimes be helpful by saying "no" or giving discipline rather than what we asked for, God must also sometimes do so to us. In our candid moments most of us will admit that the discipline, guidance and values that our parents gave us were much more valuable to us than any tangible item they gave us, even though the material things they gave us may have made us happy for the moment. So, even if we ask and God says "no" that does not mean we should stop asking of God. We should remember that God knows better than we do what are the best gifts for us.

Just as God wants us to ask, expecting that he will hear and answer our requests, he also wants us to search (or as other translations of these scriptures say, "seek") expecting that we will find. This means that we should seek God's will in all aspects of our life—our family life, our social life, our work or school life, our recreation and hobbies. There is no aspect of our lives that is outside the purview of God's interest in us. As Jesus said: "Are not two sparrows sold for a penny? Yet not one of them will fall to the ground apart from your Father. And even the hairs of your head are all counted. So do not be afraid; you are of more value than many sparrows." (Matt. 10:29-30) Just as parents are interested in even the minutiae of their children's lives, so also is God interested in our lives. He wants us to seek, believing in faith that we will find what we seek in response to God's leading. As the psalmist said, "Those who know your name put their trust in you, for you, O Lord, have not forsaken those who seek you." (Ps. 9:10)

In addition to asking and seeking, Jesus also tells us "Knock, and the door will be opened for you." A door is a metaphor for an opportunity, in this case an opportunity to serve God or to fulfill God's will in our lives. As we ask God for his will for our lives, opportunities will present themselves to us, and we must be ready to knock on that door of opportunity, believing in faith that what God has for us on the other side of the door will be wonderful. Such an opportunity is one of the good gifts that God gives us as his children. The opportunity may be a career opportunity; it may a relationship opportunity; it may be an opportunity for Christian service. But whatever the opportunity, if we have in faith sought God's will we must not be afraid to pursue what God has given to us. We should knock, knowing that the door will be opened for us.

To emphasize his point, Jesus says again "For everyone who asks receives, and everyone who searches finds, and for everyone who knocks, the door will be opened." This is the life of faith, living in such a close relationship with God, that we ask God for all our needs in life (and even some of our wants). We search his will for direction and reassurance, and welcome and embrace the opportunities that he brings to us for service, for fulfillment and for our enjoyment. Far from being a life of woodenly obeying a list of prohibitions, it is a dynamic relationship in which our Father guides us through the decisions of our lives, both large and small, and gives us the opportunity to be a participant in his plans for this wonderful but troubled world. If you are at all interested in adventure in life, you will find it in the relationship that God earnestly desires to have with you. You should expect great things because God can use simple, ordinary people like you and me to do extraordinary things if we are willing, in faith, to allow God to be involved in all aspects of our lives. He will be with us every step of the way, and where God is good things happen.

Note that it is immediately after Jesus' telling us that we should ask, seek and knock that he gives us the Golden Rule: "Do to others as you would have them do to you." In today's world it takes faith to believe in the Golden Rule. The world says "Do to others before they do to you." But that isn't what Jesus taught. Jesus commands us to treat others the way we want to be treated.

This isn't just a matter of good manners or common sense to Jesus. When the Pharisees asked Jesus which commandment in the law is the greatest, he replied:

"You shall love the Lord your God with all your heart, and with all your soul, and with all your mind. This is the greatest and first commandment. And a second is like it: You shall love your neighbor as yourself. On these two commandments hang all the law and the prophets." (Matt. 22:37-40)

How do we love our neighbor as ourselves? We treat our neighbor as we would want our neighbor to treat us. We show him compassion because we want him to show us compassion; we forgive him his sins against us just as we would want him to forgive us; we treat him with dignity and respect just as we would want to be treated. We do not hold on to any anger that may arise against him. In short, we treat him just as we want to be treated.

There is a version of the Golden Rule among the Apocryphal books of the Jews, except it is stated in the negative. In the book of Tobit, we find the words "And what you hate, do not do to anyone." (Tobit 4:15) This is certainly good advice and common sense, but what Jesus presented in the Golden Rule goes much further. Jesus is telling us that we have an affirmative duty to show compassion, to treat others with respect, to forgive them, to be generous to them, and to love them as we love ourselves. It is far different to love someone than to simply avoid hating that person.

So we must treat others just as we want to be treated. In faith, we must be obedient to our Lord in following the Golden Rule. In faith, we must believe that the world will be a better place as we treat others the way we want to be treated. In faith, we must believe that by living the Golden Rule we will bring the kingdom of heaven to our corner of the world.

The core value is:

*"I will walk in faith daily with the Lord, believing that he will lead me where I should go. And as I follow him I will treat others as I want to be treated."*

## *QUESTIONS TO CONSIDER*

1.  In this chapter we read the words of Jesus telling us to "ask" and to "search" and he tells us we will find. This requires faith. Do you have doubts about whether if you ask and search that you will find? Do you have doubts that God will give you what you ask for?

2.  In this chapter is the statement "To receive what we ask for, we must ask while living out the core values that Jesus taught." Do you agree with that statement? If we are not living the core values of Jesus do you think that might affect what we ask for?

3.  In this chapter is the statement that "Jesus promises that God will respond to our requests." Do you believe that God is responding to our requests even if we do not get precisely what we ask for? Can you think of instances in which, in retrospect, you are happy that God did *not* give you what you asked for? What are some examples of this?

4.  If God is not going to give us exactly what we ask for when we ask for it, why do you think God still wants us to ask? Do you think that our continuing to ask while prayerfully considering how God has answered our prayers will help us learn to trust God more?

5.  Do you actively seek God's will in *all* areas of you life? Are there some areas of your life for which you do not actively seek God's will? Why do you think you do not seek God's will in some areas of your life? Is there a trust problem? Is there a problem of self-centered-ness in that area of your life? What do you think you should do to open up all areas of your life to God's involvement?

6.  Do you agree with the statement in this chapter that "A door is a metaphor for an opportunity?" Have there been opportunities presented to you in your life that you have been reluctant to pursue out of fear? If you have been earnestly praying for an opportunity of some type or a solution to a problem, do you believe that you can in faith pursue that opportunity or solution to the problem? Do you

believe that pursuing such an opportunity or solution is part of the life of faith that you are to live as you abide in Christ?

7.  How well are you doing at living your life by the Golden Rule? Do you treat others as you want to be treated? In what area of your life, or with what group of people, are you least likely to do this? What is the reason for that? What can you do to overcome your tendency not to treat others as you want to be treated?

# CHAPTER 23

# THE CHALLENGE

*"Everyone then who hears these words of mine and acts on them will be like a wise man who built his house on rock. The rain fell, the floods came, and the winds blew and beat on that house, but it did not fall, because it had been founded on rock. And everyone who hears these words of mine and does not act on them will be like a foolish man who built his house on sand. The rain fell, and the floods came, and the winds blew and beat against that house, and it fell—and great was its fall." (Matt. 7:24-28)*

We end our study of the core values that Jesus taught where we began: with Jesus promising that we will be blessed if we are obedient to him and keep his commandments, and also with Jesus saying that if we expect to be blessed by him we must act on his commandments.

In the verses above, Jesus contrasts the wise man with the foolish man. Note that the wise man and the foolish man alike heard the words of Jesus. The wise man was not wise simply because he *heard* the words of Jesus. He was wise because he heard Jesus' words *and acted on them*. In other words, the values inherent in what Jesus taught became *core* values for the wise man. They were the basis upon which he made his decisions and his choices in life. Because Jesus' words became his core values, he abided in Jesus. Jesus' values were the foundation of his life, and that foundation, Jesus says, is as solid as rock.

The foolish man also heard the words of Jesus, so he had as much opportunity to develop a solid foundation as the wise man did. His problem was not that he had not heard what Jesus said, or that he failed to understand what Jesus said. His problem was that he never acted on the words that he heard. Why? There could be many reasons. He may have decided that the values Jesus taught sounded good, but he would wait until a more convenient time to live by them. He may have been unwilling to live under the discipline that obedience to Christ requires. He may have decided that Jesus' values just sounded too hard to live by. The reasons are endless, but whatever the reason, he heard what Jesus had to say, but never incorporated it into his life. He never allowed the words of Jesus to seep into his core.

For much of the time the fact that one acted on Jesus' words and the other did not seemed not to matter. But when "the rain fell, and the floods came, and the winds blew and beat against that house" it made a critical difference. The wise man's house survived; the house of the foolish man did not. It is important to note that the rain fell, the floods came and the winds blew against *both* houses. Simply because we put our faith in Jesus Christ that does not mean that we will avoid the storms of life. No matter how faithful we are in living by the core values that Jesus taught, we will still face difficulties in life similar to those who have not chosen to live by his values. But when those storms come, the wise man will be prepared to deal with them because Jesus himself is the foundation of that man's life. The foolish man will be unprepared to deal with such storms because his foundation is built on sand which the rains and floods will wash away.

I hope that by now you have begun to examine your own behavior to honestly assess whether you are living the core values that Jesus presented in the Sermon on the Mount. If you decided to read this book all the way through before beginning the exercises that I recommended in Chapter 1, I urge you to reread Chapter 1 and begin those exercises. Of course, to do the self-examination that I recommend, you will have to set aside some time each day to be alone with God for prayer, for meditation on scripture and for self-examination. If you have not yet set aside time for this each day, consider doing so immediately. Begin with at least 10 minutes and work up to 20-30 minutes each day. It will quickly become the most important part of your day.

As recommended in Chapter I, you should spend part of this time alone with the Lord examining whether you are living the core values that Jesus taught. Let's review those values:

I will always recognize that I am a sinner by nature in need of the grace and forgiveness of God—and so is everyone else. (Chapter 3)

When confronted with my own sin, I will acknowledge it, seek forgiveness and commit to change, with God's help. (Chapter 4)

I will never consider myself to be better than any other person, and will treat every person with dignity and respect. (Chapter 5)

I will at all times give my relationship with God first priority in my life. (Chapter 6)

I will always show mercy (compassion) to others and encourage others to do likewise. (Chapter 7)

I will always seek to be pure in heart and will promptly seek forgiveness when my thoughts or actions are not pure. (Chapter 8)

I will do all I can to be at peace with others and to be an agent of peace among other people. (Chapter 9)

I will not be afraid to live righteously, despite persecution, and will rejoice if I am persecuted for following him. (Chapter 10)

I will promptly release my anger before God and not hold on to it no matter what anyone does to me. (Chapter 11)

I will live a sexually pure life and avoid sexual sin. If married, I will honor and cherish my spouse and do all I can to avoid divorce. (Chapter 12)

I will always be truthful; my word is my bond. (Chapter 13)

I will not retaliate against someone who insults me or wrongs me. Instead, I will pray for that person, treat him with respect and godly love, and be generous to him if he is in need. (Chapter 14)

I will at all times strive to love my neighbor (including my enemies) as myself with the same love with which God has loved me. (Chapter 15)

I will be generous in giving to the poor, the needy and the afflicted and will avoid seeking any recognition for my giving. (Chapter 16)

I will pray regularly, following the example of Jesus. (Chapter 17)

I will promptly forgive all offenses against me, just as God has forgiven me. (Chapter 18)

I will always insure that money is my servant and not my master. (Chapter 19)

I will seek to overcome my fears and worries by placing my trust in God; I will make all decisions in life trusting him. (Chapter 20)

I will stand in judgment of no one, but I will always try to discern good and evil based upon Jesus' commandments. (Chapter 21)

I will walk in faith daily with the Lord, believing that he will lead me where I should go. And as I follow him I will treat others as I want to be treated. (Chapter 22)

As you begin to examine your own behavior in light of these values you will probably find that you do reasonably well with some of them, but you have far to go with others. Don't be discouraged. Going through the exercise of holding yourself accountable before God each day will sensitize you to your own behavior and help you change your behavior to live as Jesus taught. You will likely be surprised at how quickly your behavior, your thought life and your relationships will change.

At the same time, do not assume that this will be easy. Jesus himself told us that living in obedience to him will not be easy:

"Enter through the narrow gate; for the gate is wide and the road is easy that leads to destruction, and there are many who take it. For the gate is narrow and the road is hard that leads to life, and there are few who find it." (Matt. 7:13-14)

Why is the wide road so easy and the narrow road so hard? Because the wide road allows you to hear what Jesus said without acting on it. It allows you to go your own way, to live a largely self-centered life and do what is convenient or easy for the moment without considering the consequences. It allows you to avoid the hard choices that Jesus presented and to avoid confronting your own sins. But note that Jesus says this is the road that leads to destruction. Those on that road ignored the words of Jesus and when the storms came, their house fell because it did not have a solid foundation.

The narrow road, on the other hand, is hard. It is hard to confront our own sins and our sinful nature. It is hard to change (repent). It is hard to be humble and not to retaliate when someone insults us or unjustly criticizes us. It is hard to be merciful, to be an agent of peace rather than discord. It is hard to realize we may face some type of persecution for being obedient to Christ. It is hard to release our anger, to always be truthful, to promptly forgive those who sin against us, and to avoid being judgmental. Jesus recognizes this and bluntly tells us that the gate is narrow and the road is hard "and there are few who find it." (Matt. 7:14)

So, is it worth the effort? You will have to decide that for yourself, but note that Jesus says that the narrow road is the road "that leads to life." (Matt. 7:14) As part of that life, you will come into a loving relationship with the God who created you, who loves you and who wants what is best for you. And that will be a joyful life. The Apostle Peter, who knew of the difficulties and joys of following Jesus, described living in such a loving and joyful relationship:

> "Although you have not seen him, you love him; and even though you do not see him now, you believe in him and rejoice with an indescribable and glorious joy. For you are receiving the outcome of your faith, the salvation of your souls." (I Peter 1:8-9)

Don't you want to live a life characterized by this kind of love and joy? The only way we will be able to live in a loving relationship with God and with our brothers and sisters (our neighbors) is to accept the values that Jesus taught, to allow them to seep into the core of our being, and to hold ourselves accountable before God to live according to these values. If you do this, the words Jesus spoke to his disciples on the night before his crucifixion will apply to you:

> "As the Father has loved me, so I have loved you; abide in my love. If you keep my commandments, you will abide in my love, just as I have kept my Father's commandments and abide in his love. I have said these things to you so that my joy may be in you, and that your joy may be complete." (John 15:9-11)

## *QUESTIONS TO CONSIDER*

1. In the verses upon which this chapter is based Jesus talks about the wise man and the foolish man. The foolish man was the man who heard the words of Jesus but did not act on them. How do you think you should act on the words of Jesus so that you will not be one of the foolish men (or women)? What have you done thus far to act on the words of Jesus that we have examined in this book? What else do you plan to do?

2.  Jesus said that the foolish man built his house on sand. What do you
    think he meant by that? If the values that Jesus taught are the values
    that create a foundation of rock, what are the values that create a
    foundation of sand? How do you tell the difference in them?

3.  What is preventing you from developing the core values that Jesus
    taught so that you will have a foundation of rock in your life? When
    does Jesus say you will find out what kind of foundation you have?

4.  Have you begun examining your own behavior to honestly assess
    whether you are living the core values that Jesus taught? How are
    you doing so far? What have you learned about yourself? In what
    areas have you made the most improvement? In what areas do you
    need to improve the most?

5.  All 20 of the core values addressed in this book are listed in this
    chapter. Have you considered using this list as a checklist against
    which you will examine your behavior on a regular basis?

6.  Jesus told us that the wide road is the easy road that leads to destruc-
    tion and that the narrow road is the hard road that leads to life.
    Have you found that examining your behavior and your values on a
    regular basis is hard? Have you been tempted to stop doing it and
    return to an unexamined life? How have you dealt, or how will you
    deal, with this temptation? Have you made a commitment to
    continue examining your behavior regularly and asking God to
    change your core values to those of Jesus?

# EPILOGUE

Charles Browne served his full sentence in the state penitentiary. While he was there his wife, Carol, had to sell their house to avoid foreclosure. She was able, however, to get enough money from the sale for a down payment on a much smaller, more modest house. Carol went to work as a bank loan officer to support the family while Charles served his sentence.

While Charles was in prison he began attending a men's Bible study. For the first time Charles began to understand what it means to be a disciple of Christ. He realized that his values had not been the values Jesus expects of his followers, and he committed to change.

Upon his release from prison, Charles found a job working with at-risk teenagers to mentor them and to help them develop marketable skills. Today, he also teaches Sunday School classes for teenagers and young adults that focus on discipleship and core values.

Rachel Singleton continued to struggle financially during the recession. She did, however, find time to join a women's Bible study, and through it came to understand how her values and priorities had led her to her current circumstances. Rachel repented and committed to the Lord that she would be a faithful disciple that lived the values that Jesus taught.

About the same time that Charles was getting out of prison, Rachel received an unexpected letter from Roger. He wrote that his emotional problems from his tour in Iraq had led him into a serious drug problem. His life had not turned around until he entered a drug rehabilitation program sponsored by the Veteran's Administration. Through that program he finally overcame his drug addiction. During his rehab, he met a nurse who was a strong Christian. She led him to the Lord, and was a major reason he had remained free of drugs. They were married a year after Roger completed the rehab program.

One of the commitments that Roger made upon getting married, with his new wife's full support, was that he was going to fulfill his obligations as a father to Janie. When he learned that Janie had a sister with no father figure at home, Roger asked Rachel to allow him to be a father to Susan also. Roger began paying Rachel $500 a month in child support.

With this new source of income, Rachel was able to stop working her evening job and completed her degree. She became an elementary school teacher, which had always been her goal. Rachel also began having a family Bible study with her girls to focus on what it means to be a Christian. The girls now have the Christian core values that it took Rachel many years and much heartache to develop.

## *AUTHOR CONTACT INFORMATION*

Darryl M. Bloodworth
Post Office Box 2346
Orlando, Florida 32802-2346
www.ChristianCoreValues.com

CPSIA information can be obtained
at www.ICGtesting.com
Printed in the USA
LVOW13s1216290717
542793LV00002B/3/P

9 781932 503920